T0328781

Cambridge Elements ≡

Elements in Epistemology
edited by
Stephen Hetherington
University of New South Wales, Sydney

THE NATURE AND NORMATIVITY OF DEFEAT

Christoph Kelp
University of Glasgow

CAMBRIDGE
UNIVERSITY PRESS

Shaftesbury Road, Cambridge CB2 8EA, United Kingdom

One Liberty Plaza, 20th Floor, New York, NY 10006, USA

477 Williamstown Road, Port Melbourne, VIC 3207, Australia

314–321, 3rd Floor, Plot 3, Splendor Forum, Jasola District Centre,
New Delhi – 110025, India

103 Penang Road, #05–06/07, Visioncrest Commercial, Singapore 238467

Cambridge University Press is part of Cambridge University Press & Assessment,
a department of the University of Cambridge.

We share the University's mission to contribute to society through the pursuit of
education, learning and research at the highest international levels of excellence.

www.cambridge.org
Information on this title: www.cambridge.org/9781009161039

DOI: 10.1017/9781009161022

First published 2023

A catalogue record for this publication is available from the British Library

ISBN 978-1-009-45406-3 Hardback
ISBN 978-1-009-16103-9 Paperback
ISSN 2398-0567 (online)
ISSN 2514-3832 (print)

The Nature and Normativity of Defeat

Elements in Epistemology

DOI: 10.1017/9781009161022
First published online: August 2023

Christoph Kelp
University of Glasgow

Author for correspondence: Christoph Kelp, Christoph.kelp@glasgow.ac.uk

Abstract: Defeat is the loss of justification for believing something in light of new information. This Element mainly aims to work towards developing a novel account of defeat. It distinguishes among three broad views in the epistemology of defeat: scepticism, internalism, and externalism and argues that sceptical and internalist accounts of defeat are bound to remain unsatisfactory. As a result, any viable account of defeat must be externalist. While there is no shortage of externalist accounts, the Element provides reason to think that extant accounts remain unsatisfactory. The Element also takes on the constructive tasks of developing an alternative account of defeat and showing that it improves on the competition.

Keywords: epistemology, defeat, justification, knowledge, virtue epistemology

ISBNs: 9781009454063 (HB), ISBNs: 9781009161039 (PB), 9781009161022 (OC)
ISSNs: 2398-0567 (online), 2514-3832 (print)

Contents

1 Introduction

Suppose that you are preparing to go and see a show by your favourite band. You have bought tickets months ago and, finally, the big day has arrived. You have double- and triple-checked the dates and times. You believe that the show is happening today. Clearly, your belief is justified. Just as you are about to leave, you are notified that the show is cancelled because one of the band members has fallen ill. (In what follows, I will refer to this case as 'the cancellation case'.)

Suppose, next, that you are a detective. You have excellent evidence that a certain suspect committed the murder you are investigating: the suspect's fingerprints are on the murder weapon, their DNA is found at the crime scene, and they have an excellent motive for the deed. Based on the evidence, you come to believe that the suspect did indeed commit the crime. Again, it is hard to deny that your belief is justified. A little later, you find out that the suspect has an ironclad alibi for the time of the deed. There are eyewitnesses and video surveillance placing them at a different location ('the alibi case').

These are paradigm instances of what epistemologists call *defeat*, that is, the loss of justification for believing something in light of new information. Defeat will take centre stage in this Element. Its central aim is to work towards developing a novel account of defeat.

It is easy enough to see that achieving this aim is of considerable importance. We live in a world in which an abundance of information is just clicks away. As a result, we now have unprecedented opportunities to acquire new information. But since defeat is the loss of justification in light of new information, by the same token, we have unprecedented opportunities to acquire defeat for our justified beliefs. The expansion of our informational horizon that we have witnessed is by the same token an expansion of potential defeat for the justification of our beliefs. Many of our most deeply held beliefs about the likes of politics, religion, and ethics may be most affected. This is because the amount of information supporting claims that run contrary to our beliefs is particularly large. If these beliefs are indeed defeated, the range of our justified beliefs is much smaller than we may have thought (cf. Frances 2005). What's more, it is widely agreed that in order to permissibly assert our beliefs, we must at least have justification for them (Kelp and Simion 2021; Lackey 2008; Williamson 2000). As a result, the range of beliefs we may assert threatens to turn out to be much smaller than we may have assumed, and our practices of conducting debates about them may need to be revised dramatically. Since a viable account of defeat will offer precise conditions under which our justified beliefs suffer from defeat, such an account will be key to ascertaining how great the threat to our justified beliefs really is. What's more, it will provide an invaluable tool for understanding the extent to which we may need to revise the practices for debating our beliefs.

I said that defeat is the loss of justification for believing something in light of new information. I hope this characterisation of defeat is not only useful but also theoretically lightweight in that it is acceptable to most contributors to the debate on defeat. In fact, I think that the lightweight characterisation of defeat can be fleshed out a little further. When defeat occurs, what happens is that the new information leads to the loss of justification *by providing reason against holding certain beliefs*. In the cancellation case, the information that the show has been cancelled provides a reason against believing that the show is happening tonight. And in the alibi case, the information provided by the eyewitness testimony and surveillance videos is a reason against believing that the suspect committed the crime.

Note that in both cases, the information provides reason against holding the beliefs in question by providing reason for thinking that the beliefs are false. In the cancellation case, you acquire reason for thinking that the show is *not* happening tonight, and, in the alibi case, you acquire reason for thinking that the suspect is *not* guilty. Can we refine our lightweight characterisation of defeat by saying that what happens when defeat occurs is that new information leads to the loss of justification by providing reason for thinking that the target belief is false? No. While acquiring reason for thinking that some of our beliefs are false is one important way of acquiring defeat, it is not the only one. To see this, consider the following case.

You are looking at a surface in front of you, which looks red. Based on this, you form a belief that the surface is indeed red. This is yet another case in which your belief is justified. Shortly after, I tell you that the surface is illuminated by red light and, as a result, would look red to you even if it were white ('the illumination case').

In this case, you do not acquire a reason for thinking that your belief is false. After all, even if the surface is illuminated by red light, the question as to whether it is red remains entirely open. The table may be red illuminated by red light. Rather, what you learn is that your source, that is, visual perception, is inadequate to give you justification for believing that the surface is red. After all, visual perception doesn't allow you to tell whether it is red or white.

This is why we will do well to stick to the more inclusive characterisation of defeat in terms of information that provides a reason against holding certain beliefs. Note that this characterisation can accommodate both kinds of defeat. After all, both provide us with reason against holding some of our beliefs, one by providing reason for thinking that the beliefs are false, the other by providing reason for thinking that their sources are inadequate.[1]

Now, there is lots of new information out there that provides reason against holding various of our beliefs. Suppose someone you have never met or even heard of and who is currently in a faraway place has just asserted that your employer will be unable to pay their employees next month ('the employment case'). That someone made this assertion is information that provides reason against holding the belief that you will receive your pay as per usual. But it does not defeat the justification you have for your belief that your employer will continue to pay your salary. Why not? The answer is that for new information to defeat some justification you have, you must be related to it in the right way.

The question about this relation is one of the key divides in the epistemological debate on defeat. First, one might think that the relation is psychological (henceforth also 'the psychological view'). On this view, for new information that provides reason against holding some belief to defeat some justification one

---

[1] Consider the process reliabilist 'alternative reliable process' account of defeat (Goldman 1979; Lyons 2009). Very roughly, according to process reliabilism, whether you believe justifiably turns on whether your belief is produced via reliable cognitive processes, that is, processes that tend to produce true beliefs. And whether your justification for believing something is defeated turns on whether you have an alternative reliable process available such that were it to be used, you would not hold your belief. Crucially, defeat is explained purely in terms of processes, reasons don't feature at all here. Note also that this is no accident. Process reliabilists take pride in the fact that their account of justification is naturalistically respectable. Part of what makes it so is that it features no normative properties such as reasons. In light of this, one may wonder just how lightweight the characterisation really is.

Three comments on this. First, even though process reliabilists don't state their account of defeat in terms of reasons, it doesn't follow that their account of defeat isn't compatible with the lightweight characterisation of defeat. After all, it may be that reasons can be analysed in terms of available reliable processes. Note that, if so, the process reliabilist account achieves a nice fit with the lightweight characterisation. After all, the lightweight characterisation isn't meant as a substantive account of defeat and leaves open the possibility that the key property of reasons against believing admits of further analysis, including along process reliabilist lines. Second, defeat is a general normative phenomenon: it doesn't only occur in the epistemic domain. At the same time, it is far from clear that, in all normative domains in which defeat occurs, justification and defeat can be unpacked along process reliabilist lines. (For instance, process reliabilism is structurally a kind of rule consequentialism. While this may be plausible for the epistemic domain, it is not clear that it is equally plausible, for example, for the practical domain, which may require an act consequentialist treatment.) If it cannot, the prospects for a fully general account of defeat in terms of alternative reliable processes are dim. What's more, we may just have to revert to a general account in terms of reasons, perhaps with a process reliabilist account of what it takes to have reasons in the epistemic domain. Third, to the best of my knowledge, the alternative process account of defeat is the only account that doesn't naturally fit with the lightweight characterisation of defeat. At the same time, it has come under heavy criticism (some of which I will review in Section 3) And in order to develop a viable account of defeat, process reliabilists have started to try and make room for reasons (or something in the vicinity) in their epistemology. In light of this, no matter whether literally everyone is on board with the lightweight characterisation, I take it that it is lightweight enough to provide a useful starting point for theorising about defeat.

has for this belief is for one to stand in a to-be-specified psychological relation to the information. For instance, one could say that the relation is belief. In that case, some new information that provides reason against holding some belief defeats some justification one has only if one believes it. The reason why the assertion about your employer doesn't defeat your justification for your belief about continued pay is that you do not believe this piece of information.

The main rival to the psychological view takes the relation to be normative (henceforth also 'the normative view' (e.g. Alston 2002; Graham and Lyons 2021; Simion 2021)). On this view, for new information that provides reason against holding some belief to defeat some justification one has for this belief is for one to stand in a to-be-specified normative relation to the information. For instance, one could unpack this relation in terms of epistemic propriety to believe. In that case, some new information that provides reason against holding some belief defeats some justification one has only if it is epistemically proper for one to believe this piece of information. The reason why the assertion about your employer doesn't defeat your belief about continued pay is that it is not the case that it is epistemically proper for you to believe this piece of information.[2]

We have looked at some cases of defeat and at a lightweight characterisation of the phenomenon in terms of loss of justification in light of new information, where the new information provides reason against holding certain beliefs. With these points in play, the phenomenon that takes centre stage in this Element should now be in clear view. Before getting down to more substantive theorising about defeat, I'd like to look at some kinds of defeat that are familiar from the literature. Surveying the myriad ways in which defeat may occur will allow us to get an even better handle on the phenomenon. It will also give me the opportunity to highlight some important allegiances and flag some important assumptions that I will make in the remainder of this Element.

We have already encountered the distinction between rebutting and under-cutting defeat (e.g. Pollock 1986). Very roughly, rebutting defeat involves a reason for thinking that some belief we hold is false (the cancellation and alibi cases), and undercutting defeat involves a reason for thinking that the source of some beliefs is inadequate (the illumination case). The distinction between undercutting and rebutting defeat is widely endorsed in the literature and I will take it on board for present purposes.

---

[2] Note that it is possible to have a conjunctive view on which the relation must be both psychological and normative (e.g. what's needed is belief that it is epistemically proper for one to hold), or a disjunctive view on which a psychological relation is sufficient, and a normative relation is also sufficient.

Another important distinction is between misleading and non-misleading defeat. Very roughly, misleading defeat involves information that provides reason against holding a certain belief by providing evidence for a falsehood. To see what I have in mind, consider a version of the illumination case in which my statement that the surface is illuminated by red light is a lie. In fact, the light shining on the surface is standard white light. Or consider a version of the cancellation case in which the notification that the show is cancelled is sent by mistake. In fact, the show is going ahead as planned. In both cases, the defeaters you acquire are misleading. In the tweaked illumination case, my testimony provides reason against believing that the surface is red by providing evidence for a falsehood, to wit, that the surface is illuminated by red light. Likewise, in the tweaked cancellation case, the notification you receive provides reason against believing that the show is happening tonight by providing evidence for a falsehood, to wit, that the show was cancelled.

Most contributors to the debate register an intuition that there is such a thing as misleading defeat. For instance, they maintain that, in the tweaked illumination and cancellation cases, intuitively, you lose justification for your beliefs in light of misleading defeaters. In fact, most contributors to the debate also register an intuition that you can even lose knowledge via misleading defeat. For instance, in the tweaked illumination and cancellation cases, it may well be that initially your beliefs qualified as knowledge. Even so, once the new information comes in, you lose your justification and, indeed, your knowledge as a result of misleading defeaters. While I will look at views that take at least knowledge to be indefeasible in Section 1, for now I'd like to flag that I side with the majority here in that I take it that justification and knowledge admit of defeat even via misleading defeaters.

The next distinction I'd like to highlight is between justification defeaters and (pure) knowledge defeaters. The most important idea here is that, alongside the class of justification defeaters we have already familiarised ourselves with, there is a class of defeaters that only target knowledge, leaving the justification of our beliefs intact. (Pure) knowledge defeaters have been of particular interest for champions of defeasibility accounts of knowledge, which aim to solve the Gettier (1963) problem by invoking defeat (e.g. Lehrer and Paxson 1969; Swain 1974). To get an idea of how this is meant to work, consider a standard Gettier case. You acquire a justified true belief that it's 8:22 by taking a reading from your watch. Crucially, unbeknownst to you, your wristwatch stopped exactly twelve hours ago ('the stopped clock case'). In this case, your justified true belief that it's 8:22 falls short of knowledge. According to defeasibility accounts of knowledge, the reason for this has to do with defeat. More specifically, the thought is that the fact that your clock is stopped defeats your knowledge that it's 8:22.

Of course, if this project can be made to work, my characterisation of defeat requires reworking. To see why, note that I characterise defeat in terms of loss of justification. If defeasibility theorists are right, then there is defeat of knowledge without defeat of justification. And, of course, if that's correct, any characterisation of defeat in terms of loss of justification cannot be adequate. Now, I do not mean to foreclose the possibility of (pure) knowledge defeat. That said, for present purposes, I'd like to set it aside and restrict my focus to justification defeat. By the same token, any problem that the existence of knowledge defeat may cause for my characterisation of defeat in terms of loss of justification can safely be ignored.

The last distinction I'd like to look at is perhaps the most controversial. This is the distinction between internal and external defeat.[3] While, in cases of internal defeat, the defeater is psychologically registered by the relevant believer, in cases of external defeat it isn't.[4] One may wonder why I say that this distinction is controversial. After all, if there is such a thing as (pure) knowledge defeat as defeasibility theorists would have us think, then there must also be such a thing as external defeat. After all, the kinds of (pure) knowledge defeaters that would explain the absence of knowledge in Gettier cases are standardly not psychologically registered. For instance, in the stopped clock case, the fact that your wristwatch is stopped, which constitutes the (pure) knowledge defeater here, is not psychologically registered.

I agree that once we allow for (pure) knowledge defeaters, then we will also have to countenance external defeat. What I mean when I say that the distinction between internal and external defeat is controversial is that it is controversial that there is such a thing as external defeat of justification (henceforth just 'external defeat'). That is to say, what is controversial is that we can lose justification for believing something in light of information that we do not psychologically register. Note that all cases of (justification) defeat we have encountered so far are cases of internal defeat. In all cases you register the relevant information that provides reasons against holding the relevant beliefs. For instance, in the cancellation case, you learn about the cancellation, and, in the alibi case, you find out about the eyewitness testimony and the video surveillance. What's more, it may be hard to see how information that we don't register could lead to the defeat of justification. For

---

[3] Note that the phenomenon sometimes goes by the labels 'propositional defeat' (Bergmann 2006) or 'normative defeat' (e.g. Lackey 2008). I am not happy with either term. The first suggests an analogy with propositional justification. Propositional justification is something that internalists can and indeed happily do acknowledge the existence of. The existence of what I call external defeat is incompatible with internalism. This is why I prefer not to go with 'propositional defeat' as a label. Normative defeat suggests that there is also non-normative defeat. Again, I take it that this is false, which is why I am not satisfied with this label either. That said, nothing hinges on this choice of terminology.

[4] What does it take for a defeater, d, to be psychologically registered? For present purposes, I follow Lackey (e.g. 1999, 2003) in that one needs to have some doxastic attitude towards d (like beliefs or doubt).

instance, how could your justification for believing that the show is happening tonight be defeated if you never received the notification that it was cancelled? And how could your justification for believing that the suspect is guilty be defeated if the information about the alibi and the video surveillance never got through to you?

What's more, things don't look much more promising when we look at the classical cases of external defeat in the literature. Here is one. Suppose I want to play a prank on you and make you believe that I am in San Francisco for the summer, while, really, I am in Rome. To this end, I mail a bunch of letters with descriptions of my stay in San Francisco to a friend in San Francisco who mails them from San Francisco to you. At present they are in a pile of unopened letters on your desk that has been accumulating for days. You happen to call my office and are told that I am spending the summer in Rome ('the unopened letter case', Harman 1980, 164).

The thought here is that the fact that the letters on your desk say that I am in San Francisco constitutes a defeater. While originally the case was meant as a case of defeat of knowledge, it is sometimes considered a case of defeat of justification also (Nottelmann 2021, 1185). I agree that it is not clear that this is a genuine case of defeat. Even the claim that it is a case in which knowledge is defeated strikes me as tenuous. The claim that it is a case of justification defeat is more controversial.

In light of this, it becomes more and more understandable why the distinction between internal and external defeat has remained controversial. Even so, one key ambition of this Element is to mount a case that there is such a thing as external defeat and that, as a result, any adequate epistemology of defeat must make room for external defeat. Accordingly, one of the central tasks for the account of defeat I am to develop is to show how this can be done.

Note that the case for external defeat has implications for the debate between the psychological view and the normative view. To see this, recall that cases of external defeat involve defeaters that aren't psychologically registered. This means that, in cases of external defeat, the kind of relation that the psychological view posits doesn't obtain. As a result, if there is such a thing as external defeat, the psychological view cannot be correct.[5] Unsurprisingly, I favour a version of the normative view. Accordingly, another central task for this Element, which I take on in Section 5, is to develop a version of the normative view that can allow

---

[5] That said, for present purposes, I don't need to take a stance on whether some psychological relation is sufficient for a defeater to undermine justification. What matters is that no psychological relation is required for this. After all, that's what is needed to make room in our epistemology for external defeat. Accordingly, for present purposes, the correct view may well be a hybrid one. That said, I worry that the psychological view overgenerates defeat. Sexists may have defeaters for the word of women simply in virtue of the fact that they believe that women are not trustworthy. In my view, this can't be right. Defeat cannot be that easy to come by. In light of this, I will take it that the normative view is correct here.

for external defeat without overgenerating defeat. For instance, in the employment case, we will want the view to predict that your belief that you will continue to receive your pay continues to be justified (i.e. not defeated) even after some stranger in a faraway place has asserted that your employer will be unable to pay their employees next month.

Here is a game plan for this Element. I distinguish among three broad views in the epistemology of defeat: scepticism, internalism, and externalism. I argue that there is excellent reason to think that sceptical and internalist accounts of defeat remain unsatisfactory. More specifically, I argue, *pace* sceptics, that we do need to countenance defeat in epistemology (Section 1). *Pace* internalists, I provide reason to believe that the correct epistemology of defeat must be externalist. The perhaps most important reason for this, albeit not the only one, is that the correct epistemology of defeat must countenance the existence of external defeat (Section 2). As a result, any viable account of defeat must be externalist. While externalists have the resources to accommodate external defeat in principle, I argue that extant externalist accounts have failed to successfully accommodate external defeat in practice. The reason for this is that externalist accounts of defeat are either too restrictive or too inclusive (Section 3). Finally, I begin to develop a better alternative. More specifically, I introduce my preferred account of justification and develop an account of defeat for it, which, I argue, can handle not only familiar cases of internal defeat (Section 4) but also the particularly difficult cases of external defeat (Section 5).

2 Defeat Scepticism

2.1 Introduction

Sceptics about defeat think that there is no such thing as defeat. To be fair, sceptics about defeat typically focus on knowledge and hold that knowledge does not admit of defeat. In this way, defeat sceptics may not be all that radical after all. Even so, if it turns out that a central epistemic property is indefeasible, that's an interesting result in its own right. What's more, it does raise the question whether defeat scepticism generalises beyond knowledge. After all, as we have seen in the Introduction, intuitively knowledge does admit of defeat. If defeat sceptics are right and this intuition is mistaken, we have to take seriously the possibility that we make a similar mistake in cases in which, intuitively, justification is defeated.

The central aim of this section is to argue against defeat scepticism. More specifically, I will provide reason to believe that the perhaps most prominent general argument for defeat scepticism fails (Section 1.2).[6] More importantly

---

[6] Note that there are also more modest approaches which aim to defend scepticism about specific kinds of defeat (e.g. defeat via higher-order evidence, see e.g. Coates 2012; Lasonen-Aarnio 2014;

yet, if defeat scepticism is to be viable at all, its advocates will need an alternative explanation of what's going on in intuitive cases of defeat; that is, they need an error theory. Section 1.3 takes a closer look at the two main error theories in the literature. I argue that one ultimately doesn't succeed in making do without defeat. While the other one is more promising, I argue that if it is successful, it can be used, and indeed is better used, as a non-sceptical account of defeat. Finally, Section 1.4 argues that there is reason to think that the more promising account doesn't work in any case, no matter whether it is used as an error theory by defeat sceptics or as a non-sceptical account of defeat.

2.2 The Case for Defeat Scepticism

Let's begin by taking a look at why one might think that knowledge does not admit of defeat. The most popular answer is that our best accounts of knowledge do not appear to allow for the possibility of defeat. Maria Lasonen-Aarnio (2010) argues this point forcefully for safety accounts of knowledge, which are among the leading accounts of knowledge on the market.[7]

The core idea of safety accounts of knowledge is that knowledge is belief that is safe from error, where safety from error is a matter of avoiding error across nearby possible worlds. It is widely agreed that this core idea needs refinement. In particular, the safety condition on knowledge needs to be relativised to ways in which the relevant belief is held. While there are several ways of making this idea more precise, I'll be working with the following rough view: One's belief that p is safe if and only if there are no nearby worlds at which one holds a false belief on whether p in the same way.[8]

To get a feeling for how the view works, let's consider a couple of cases. I know that there is a laptop in front of me. Here my belief that there is a laptop in front of me is safe. After all, it is held via my ability to recognise laptops and there are no nearby worlds at which this ability delivers a false belief on whether there is a laptop in front of me. Contrast this case with a standard Gettier case such as the stopped clock case. Recall that, in this case, you acquire a justified

---

Wedgwood 2012). Due to limitations of space, I will not look at these approaches here. Instead, I will focus entirely on approaches that aim to establish a more general form of defeat scepticism.

[7] For a similar line of argument see Baker-Hytch and Benton (2015). An alternative route to defeat scepticism is to go for an account of knowledge on which knowledge is very easy to get. One example here is the view that knowledge is just true belief (e.g. Sartwell 1992), or at least that minimal knowledge is (e.g. Hetherington 2001). It's hard to see how knowledge could be defeated on this kind of view (though of course it can be lost via loss of belief). I will not take the time to discuss this kind of view here. The main reason for this is that I think this kind of view fails for reasons unrelated to defeat (see e.g. Turri 2012).

[8] Prominent defences of safety accounts of knowledge include Pritchard (2005); Sosa (1999); Williamson (2000), for criticisms see, for example, Comesaña (2005); Kelp (2009); Neta and Rohrbaugh (2004).

true belief that it is 8:22 by taking a reading from your stopped wristwatch. Here, too, your belief that it is 8:22 is held via your ability to read the clock. Crucially, here your belief is not safe. There are nearby worlds at which you look at your wristwatch a minute earlier or later. Since at those worlds, your watch is still stopped, it does not display the right time and you end up with a false belief that it is 8:22.

Now, in a nutshell, the trouble is that the question as to whether a belief is safe does not turn on whether one has a defeater in the way we'd need it to. To see this, consider the following case. My nephew is accused of a crime. I have ample evidence that he is innocent, and I believe that he is innocent ('the nephew case'). Now consider two ways of developing this case. In the first, my belief that my nephew is innocent is held based on careful consideration of the evidence I have. Here my belief is safe (or so we may assume). After all, there are no nearby worlds at which I hold my belief on whether my nephew is innocent via careful consideration of the evidence, and yet I end up with a false belief. Safety accounts deliver the desired result that my belief qualifies as knowledge. In the second, despite all the evidence that I have, my belief that my nephew is innocent is held via a coin toss. Here my belief is unsafe. After all, at many nearby worlds at which I form a belief on whether my nephew is innocent based on a coin toss, I don't get lucky and end up with a false belief. Again, safety accounts deliver the desired result.

For present purposes, the important take home lesson concerns the key relativisation to ways of holding beliefs at issue in the safety condition. How a given belief is held is independent from what evidence one has. Rather, it is a contingent matter of psychological fact. In particular, even if one has excellent evidence for believing a certain proposition, the question of whether one's belief qualifies as knowledge remains open. If one holds one's belief via careful consideration of the evidence (as in the first development of the nephew case), it may count as knowledge. However, there just isn't any guarantee that one will hold one's belief in this way. In fact, it may well be that one holds one's belief in a different way, one that prevents it from qualifying as knowledge (as the second development of the nephew case clearly indicates).[9]

With these points in play, let's return to the question as to why safety accounts will struggle to accommodate standard cases of defeat. To see the answer, recall one of our toy examples from the Introduction, the illumination case. More specifically, consider a version of the case in which I know that the surface in front of me is red. According to safety accounts, this is because I have a safe

---

[9] These points are familiar from the literature on propositional and doxastic justification. The distinction dates back to Firth (1978). For more on propositional and doxastic justification see, for example, Silva and Oliveira (2022).

belief that it is red. The way in which my belief is held, via my ability to recognise colours from the way they look, say, does not lead me into error across nearby possible worlds. Now suppose that you tell me that the surface is white but cleverly illuminated by red light to look red.

Now suppose that what we want to say about this case is that my knowledge that the surface is red is defeated. The trouble for safety accounts is that they will struggle to do so in a satisfactory manner. In particular, consider a development of the case in which I continue to hold my belief that the surface is red via my ability to recognise colours from the way they look. Since how my belief is held is a contingent matter of psychological fact and independent of the evidence I have, there is every reason to think that this will be possible. But if this is how I hold my belief, then my belief continues to be safe. After all, it continues to be the case that the way in which my belief is held, that is, via my ability to recognise colours from the way they look, will not lead me into error across nearby possible worlds.

The above argument targets only one specific account of knowledge. Lasonen-Aarnio acknowledges this point but also notes that the discussion still serves to bring out the kinds of problem that externalist accounts of defeat will face. As will become clear in due course, she is right about this in that the kind of problem is one that we will encounter again further down the line (e.g. Section 4).

Of course, Lasonen-Aarnio's argument is far from conclusive. There may well be a viable account of knowledge that also allows for a viable account of defeat. In fact, it is one of the central ambitions of this Element to develop one. That said, for now I'd like to focus on defeat scepticism. And to be more precise, I'd like to take a closer look at what, according to defeat sceptics, is going on in paradigm cases of defeat. Unsurprisingly, defeat sceptics offer an error theory for paradigm cases of defeat. That is to say, while these cases appear to be cases of defeat, they really aren't. Something else is happening here that explains why we are misled into thinking that these cases are cases of defeat. There are two prominent versions of this error theory. In what follows, I will look at both and argue that they remain ultimately unsatisfactory.

2.3 Error Theories

Let's begin with the first strategy. The key idea here is that the relevant paradigm cases of defeat are cases in which we do have knowledge, but the probability that we know on our evidence turns out to be low. For instance, in the version of the illumination case we are now considering, I know that the surface in front of me is red. What happens when you tell me that the surface is white but cleverly illuminated by red light to look red is this. While I retain my knowledge that the surface is red, the probability on my evidence that I know that the surface is red is now low. The reason why, in paradigm cases of defeat, we think that we do not have knowledge is that we mistake the low probability of knowledge for its absence.[10]

Unfortunately, the prospects for this strategy are rather dim. To see this, note that we may easily describe the case as one in which, initially, I not only know that the surface in front of me is red, but I also know that the probability on my evidence that I know that it is red is high. If, as a result of your testimony, the probability on my evidence that I know that the surface is red is now low, it follows that my knowledge that the probability on my evidence that I know that the surface is red is high is now lost in light of the new information, that is, your testimony.[11] But that is just to say that your testimony defeated my knowledge that the probability on my evidence that I know that the surface is red is high.

This means that this strategy is not available to defeat sceptics for the simple reason that it doesn't allow defeat sceptics to make do without knowledge defeat after all. This is because they need to allow for defeat of knowledge of what's probable on our evidence, at least in certain cases. But then they need an account of defeat. And, of course, they will also encounter the problem of squaring this account with a viable account of knowledge. What's more, in that case, the motivation for treating paradigm cases of defeat by means of an error theory is significantly diminished. By the same token, the motivations for adopting scepticism about defeat are diminished also.

Perhaps the second strategy fares better. The key idea here is that, in the relevant paradigm cases of defeat, we do have knowledge, at least if we continue to believe in the same way as before. At the same time, our beliefs are unreasonable in that they manifest bad epistemic dispositions, where a bad epistemic disposition is, roughly, a disposition that leads us to form beliefs with an unfavourable knowledge to ignorance ratio.[12] For instance, in our toy example, I know that the surface before me is red even after you told me that it is white and cleverly illuminated to look red. However, I manifest the bad epistemic disposition of *believing that the surface is red via my ability to recognise colours from the way they look whilst having evidence that my colour vision is not to be trusted.* In this way, while I continue to know, my belief is unreasonable. The reason why we think that we do not have knowledge here is that we mistake the unreasonableness of the belief for the absence of knowledge.

As a first observation, note that this strategy, too, allows for some kind of defeat. To see this, note that we may assume that, initially, my belief that the

---

[10] Williamson pursues this kind of strategy in Williamson (2009, 315).

[11] After all, by the factivity of knowledge, if that probability is low, then I don't know that it is high.

[12] This is Lasonen-Aarnio's (e.g. 2010) strategy.

surface is red not only qualified as knowledge but was also reasonable. After all, it did manifest good epistemic dispositions, ones that lead us to form beliefs with a favourable knowledge to ignorance ratio, that is, the disposition of believing that the surface is red via my ability to recognise colours from the way they look. If, as a result of your testimony, my belief is now held via bad epistemic dispositions, what happens is that the reasonableness of my belief is lost in light of new information. But this is just to say that your testimony defeated the reasonableness of my belief.[13]

One might wonder whether once we acknowledge that reasonableness admits of defeat, we might not have gone a good way towards conceding that the same goes for knowledge. After all, isn't all that we need now the widely accepted claim that knowledge entails reasonable belief? Not quite. After all, it may be that there are further conditions on knowledge, which exclude the possibility of defeat of reasonableness for beliefs that count as knowledge. What does come dangerously close to having to concede that knowledge admits of defeat is allowing, in addition, that there are cases of knowledge in which one's belief is no longer reasonable due to defeat. After all, in that case, it is precisely not the case that there are further conditions on knowledge that exclude the possibility of defeat of reasonableness for beliefs that count as knowledge. Unsurprisingly, Lasonen-Aarnio is entirely aware of this issue. She addresses it by arguing that knowledge does not entail reasonable belief, that is, that it is possible to know something even though one's underlying belief is unreasonable (2010, 12).

In this way, Lasonen-Aarnio's defence of defeat scepticism rests crucially on the claim that knowledge does not entail reasonable belief. If it turns out that

---

[13] There may be other problems with this strategy. For instance, if Lasonen-Aarnio is right and reasonable belief is a matter of believing via good epistemic dispositions, and if how a belief is held is a contingent matter of psychological fact, it should be possible that, in putative cases of defeat, I continue to hold my belief via the good disposition. In that case, the belief continues to be reasonable. But, of course, this is bad news for Lasonen-Aarnio's error theory. After all, if the target belief isn't unreasonable, the prospects of accounting for the intuition of defeat in terms of mistaking unreasonableness for absence of knowledge are dim. While I will return to this problem in Section 1.4, I will set it aside for now. Instead, I will assume that the error theory works as envisaged. This should be unproblematic, at least for present purposes, because my main aim here is to argue that if Lasonen-Aarnio's error theory works, we have reason to favour an alternative view that allows for knowledge defeat. Of course, if Lasonen-Aarnio's error theory doesn't work, we don't have reason to think that the alternative view works. But that's fine at this stage of the dialectic. After all, in that case, we also have the result that Lasonen-Aarnio's view remains unsatisfactory.

A complication is that the alternative view is a virtue epistemological account of knowledge of the sort that I want to defend in this Element. This means that if Lasonen-Aarnio faces a problem here, then so does the kind of view that I want to defend. Even so, there is no need to address this problem just now. Instead, I will defer discussion of how virtue epistemology can deal with this problem until Section 4, where I discuss virtue epistemological views in more detail.

knowledge does entail reasonable belief and if her story about how reasonable belief is lost in the relevant paradigm cases of defeat checks out, then Lasonen-Aarnio should acknowledge that we have a viable account of defeat for knowledge after all, that is, her account now understood as an account of how reasonableness of belief admits of defeat. So, let's ask how plausible the claim that knowledge doesn't entail reasonable belief really is.

Lasonen-Aarnio offers a theoretical argument for the existence of unreasonable knowledge. The key thought is that, in general, the question as to whether a certain attempt is successful is independent of the question of whether it was produced by good dispositions to attain it (2010, 17). For instance, an archer's shot may be successful in that it hits the target, even though it was produced via bad dispositions (e.g. whilst drunk or blindfolded). As a result, we should expect knowledge to follow suit. In particular, we should expect that it's possible to have knowledge even though one's belief was produced by bad epistemic dispositions. If so, we should expect there to be unreasonable knowledge. If we don't, we are committed to a problematic form of exceptionalism about knowledge, according to which knowledge behaves differently from other kinds of normative phenomena.

Unfortunately, Lasonen-Aarnio's argument does not quite succeed. In a nutshell, here is why. First, there are views of knowledge according to which knowledge requires reasonable belief in Lasonen-Aarnio's sense, that is, belief that is held via good epistemic dispositions. Second, at least some of these views aren't committed to any problematic form of exceptionalism about knowledge.

The view of knowledge I have in mind is virtue epistemology.[14] Very roughly, virtue epistemology endorses a normative framework for the assessments of attempts that countenances three normative categories: success, competence, and aptness. Here an attempt is successful if and only if it attains its aim; it is competent if and only if it is produced by an ability to succeed, that is, by a good disposition; and it is apt if and only if it is successful because competent, that is, successful because produced by a good disposition (e.g. Sosa 2021). Moreover, virtue epistemology takes belief to be a kind of attempt. More specifically, according to the standard version of virtue epistemology, a belief is a kind of attempt that aims at truth.[15] This means that belief can be assessed in terms of the normative categories of success, competence, and aptness. Note also that since belief aims at truth, a belief is successful if and

---

[14] The most prominent champions of this view are Ernest Sosa (e.g. 2021), John Greco (e.g. 2010), and Linda Zagzebski (e.g. 1996).

[15] There are alternative versions of this view according to which belief doesn't aim at truth but at knowledge. I will return to this issue in Section 4.

only if it is true. The last piece of the puzzle is that standard virtue epistemology identifies familiar epistemic properties with normative properties of beliefs as attempts. In particular, standard virtue epistemology identifies justified/ reasonable belief with competent belief and knowledge with apt belief.

Note that according to standard virtue epistemology, a belief is reasonable if and only if it is produced by an epistemic ability, that is, by a good epistemic disposition. In this way, standard virtue epistemology vindicates Lasonen-Aarnio's account of reasonable belief. In addition, since knowledge is apt belief, knowledge is belief that is true because competent. In other words, knowledge is belief that is true because produced by a good epistemic disposition, that is, true because reasonable. In this way, we can see that there is a view, standard virtue epistemology, on which knowledge entails reasonable belief in Lasonen-Aarnio's sense. This completes the first part of my argument.

The second part of the argument is to provide reason to think that standard virtue epistemology isn't committed to any problematic form of exceptionalism about knowledge. To this end, let's start by returning to Lasonen-Aarnio's theoretical argument. Her key point was that, in general, the question as to whether a certain attempt is successful is independent of the question of whether it was produced by good dispositions. Just as an archer's shot may hit the target, even though it was produced via bad archery dispositions, so a belief may qualify as knowledge even though it was produced by bad epistemic dispositions. To deny this is to commit to a problematic form of exceptionalism about knowledge, according to which knowledge behaves differently from other kinds of normative phenomena.

Now, Lasonen-Aarnio is right that it is entirely possible for an attempt to be successful and not competent. For instance, it is entirely possible for an archer's shot to hit the target even when produced by bad dispositions. And it is, of course, also possible for us to form beliefs that are successful even when they are produced by bad dispositions.

However, this does not commit standard virtue epistemology to the view that we can have knowledge even when our beliefs are produced by bad epistemic dispositions, nor to a problematic exceptionalism about knowledge.

To see this, recall first that standard virtue epistemology identifies successful belief with true belief. Crucially, second, standard epistemology does not identify successful belief with knowledge. Instead, third, it identifies knowledge with apt belief.

Since standard virtue epistemology identifies successful belief with true belief, it can allow that beliefs that are produced by bad epistemic dispositions can be successful. After all, it can allow that beliefs produced by bad epistemic dispositions can be true.

Since standard virtue epistemology does not identify successful belief with knowledge, the fact that, in general, successful attempts can be produced by bad dispositions provides no reason to think that it should be possible for knowledge to be produced by bad epistemic dispositions.

Finally, since standard virtue epistemology identifies knowledge with apt belief and since, in general, apt attempts must be produced by good dispositions, standard virtue epistemology isn't committed to a problematic exceptionalism about knowledge. On the contrary, knowledge behaves in exactly the same way as other forms of apt attempt.

Let's take stock. Recall that Lasonen-Aarnio's case for defeat scepticism turns centrally on the claim that knowledge doesn't entail reasonable belief and that she offers a theoretical argument for this claim: to say otherwise is to commit to a problematic form of exceptionalism about knowledge. We have now seen that this argument doesn't go through. There is a view, standard virtue epistemology, on which knowledge does entail reasonable belief in Lasonen-Aarnio's sense and that is not committed to any form of exceptionalism about knowledge.

Where does this leave us? Part of the answer is that Lasonen-Aarnio's argument for defeat scepticism remains unsuccessful. Now, we might think that this leaves the question of whether defeat scepticism is true wide open. However, on reflection, it is not so clear that this is correct. There is now theoretical reason for thinking that defeat scepticism is false, at least at the current stage in the dialectic. To see this, let's suppose once more that Lasonen-Aarnio's treatment of the relevant paradigm cases of defeat works in that she is right that the beliefs in these cases are no longer reasonable. Let's also grant that her explanation of why they are no longer reasonable is successful. As I already noted, this means that she allows for defeat of reasonableness and indeed offers an account of defeat for reasonableness of belief. What we have seen above is that, if successful, this account can be used by champions of virtue epistemology to explain not only defeat of reasonableness, but also defeat of knowledge. In contrast, according to Lasonen-Aarnio, there is no defeat of knowledge here, and she offers an error theory for those who think that there is, where this error theory de facto is an account of defeat of reasonableness.

Let's compare the two package deals. On the one hand, we have virtue epistemology, which allows us to hold on to the plausible claim that knowledge entails reasonable belief (without incurring a commitment to a problematic exceptionalism about knowledge), offers a unified account of defeat for knowledge and reasonable belief, and avoids error theories as well as defeat scepticism. On the other hand, we have Lasonen-Aarnio's view, according to which knowledge doesn't entail reasonable belief, knowledge is unlike most other normative properties, including epistemic ones (reasonableness of belief), in that it is not defeasible, and we are committed to an error theory as well as defeat scepticism. There can little doubt that, between these two options, Lasonen-Aarnio's is the less attractive one, on theoretical grounds. Her competition offers a view that scores higher on several theoretical virtues, including prior plausibility, uniformity, and elegance. By the same token, there is theoretical reason for thinking that defeat scepticism is false, or, at the very least, that Lasonen-Aarnio's version of it is.

2.4 Defeat Despite Good Dispositions

The last question I'd like to consider in this section concerns the viability of Lasonen-Aarnio's error theory. This question will be important even if we set the issue between standard virtue epistemology and Lasonen-Aarnio's defeat scepticism aside for a moment. After all, even if Lasonen-Aarnio comes out on top, her version of defeat scepticism will work only if her error theory is indeed viable. On the other hand, if standard virtue epistemology is preferable, whether Lasonen-Aarnio's view works as an account of defeat of reasonableness is also of key importance to whether what we end up with is a viable account of defeat in the first place.

Recall that, according to Lasonen-Aarnio, a reasonable belief is one that manifests good epistemic dispositions, where a good epistemic disposition is one that produces beliefs with a favourable knowledge to ignorance ratio. Let's grant that someone who believes via a bad epistemic disposition does not believe reasonably. Now, recall that it's entirely possible for someone to have a belief that is held via good epistemic dispositions until the point at which the defeater comes in. For instance, in the illumination case, my belief that the surface before me is red is initially held via good dispositions. We may assume not only that it qualifies as knowledge, but also that it is reasonable. When you tell me that the surface is illuminated by red light, my belief ceases to be reasonable. This means that it is no longer held via a good epistemic disposition. Rather, according to Lasonen-Aarnio, it is now held via a bad epistemic disposition, for example, the disposition to believe that the surface is red via my ability to recognise colours from the way they look whilst having evidence that my colour vision is not to be trusted.

But now recall that we saw earlier (Section 1.2) that how a belief is held is a contingent matter of psychological fact. If so, we might wonder why it must be that the way the belief is held must change from a good way to a bad way, and why it could not continue to be held in a good way.

Here is an answer that one might give on behalf of Lasonen-Aarnio. Suppose one has adopted a general disposition to respond dogmatically in the face of defeat in that, as a result, one is generally disposed to hold on to one's belief even when one has evidence that it is false or that the way in which it is held is not to be trusted on the occasion in question. If one has indeed adopted this disposition, then it is only natural to think that the case at hand is a manifestation of this disposition and hence that the way in which one's belief is held is now bad, even if it had been held in a good way before.

The trouble is that there are cases of defeat that don't fit the bill. We can imagine that one has adopted the general disposition to respond non-dogmatically in the face of defeat in that one is disposed to revise one's beliefs when one has evidence that it is false or that the way in which it is held is not to be trusted on the occasion in question. However, we are fallible agents. While our good epistemic dispositions are reliable, they are not infallible. This means that they may fail to manifest on certain occasions. Now consider a case in which, while one has the general disposition to respond non-dogmatically to defeat, this disposition doesn't manifest on the occasion in question, and one holds on to one's belief instead. For instance, suppose I came to know via testimony that, last Tuesday, Paul was at the office all day, and now I know it via memory. Suppose that you overheard the episode and want to correct what you take to be a false belief I acquired. So, only a few moments later, you tell me that you saw Paul Christmas shopping in town last Tuesday afternoon. (Of course, you are wrong here: the person you saw was someone else who looks just like Paul.) Even though I am generally disposed to respond non-dogmatically to defeat, on this occasion, this disposition fails to manifest. As a result, I continue to believe that Paul was at the office all day. If there is defeat of knowledge, my testimonial-memorial knowledge that Paul was in the office all day on Tuesday is now defeated. By the same token, if Lasonen-Aarnio's error theory is correct, my belief that Paul was in the office all day on Tuesday is no longer reasonable; that is, it is no longer held via good epistemic dispositions.

The problem for Lasonen-Aarnio is that an explanation of what's happening here in terms of a bad epistemic disposition to remain dogmatic in the face of defeat is unpromising. After all, the case is one in which I have the opposite disposition, that is, the disposition to respond non-dogmatically to defeat (although, of course, this disposition fails to manifest). I simply don't have the disposition to remain dogmatic in the face of belief.[16] But given that an

---

[16] To say that I also have the disposition to respond dogmatically to defeat and that the case manifests that disposition would be a mistake. The only principled way to make this work is by holding that all behaviour is the manifestation of a corresponding disposition. If this isn't immediately obvious, note that if there are some cases in which a piece of behaviour is not the

explanation in terms of bad epistemic dispositions doesn't work, since it is contingent how a belief is held, we may expect it to be possible for me to continue to hold my belief about Paul via good epistemic dispositions. And while the possibility claim is really all that is needed here, it may be worth noting that, in this case, it is independently plausible that I do actually continue to hold my belief via good epistemic dispositions. After all, it is independently plausible that I continue to hold my belief in the same way as I did before I acquired the defeater, that is, via a combination of testimony and memory. And we have already seen that these are epistemically good dispositions.

What comes to light is that even though Lasonen-Aarnio's error theory can accommodate an important range of cases of defeat, that is, cases in which the agent has a general bad epistemic disposition to remain dogmatic in the face of defeat, it cannot accommodate the full range of such cases. In particular, her account fails in cases in which agents acquire defeaters but do not have bad epistemic dispositions to respond dogmatically to defeat.[17]

2.5 Conclusion

This section has focused on defeat scepticism. I have outlined the perhaps most promising way of arguing for scepticism about defeat for knowledge, the key idea of which is that our best accounts of knowledge don't appear to have the resources to allow for defeat.

Of course, if scepticism about defeat is to be defensible at all, its champions will need a way of accounting for the intuition that there is defeat of knowledge. One prominent view here is that we are mistaking low probability of knowledge on one's evidence for absence of knowledge. However, this strategy doesn't work because cases of defeat may involve knowledge of high probability of knowledge on one's evidence, at least initially, with the result that there must be at least defeat of some knowledge.

The other strategy aims to analyse cases of defeat as cases of unreasonable knowledge, that is, cases in which knowledge is held via bad epistemic dispositions. I argued that there are at least two reasons for thinking that this strategy remains unsuccessful. First, if the strategy works, it can be redeployed by standard virtue epistemology to offer a non-sceptical account of defeat, which, all things considered, compares favourably with its sceptical rival.

---

manifestation of a corresponding disposition, it is unclear why we can't stipulate that the case at hand is a case in point. But to hold that all behaviour is the manifestation of a corresponding disposition threatens to trivialise explanations of behaviour in terms of dispositions.

[17] By the same token, there is reason to think that we cannot offer a viable account of defeat by incorporating Lasonen-Aarnio's account of defeat of reasonableness into a virtue epistemology.

Second, there is reason to think that the strategy doesn't work after all because there are cases of defeat in which no bad epistemic dispositions are manifested.

3 Internalism and Defeat

3.1 Introduction

This section focuses on internalist accounts of defeat. Let's begin with a brief characterisation of two forms of internalism that will be of importance in this section. The first, which I will call 'internalism in epistemology', is the view that epistemic justification strongly supervenes on the internal in that any two possible agents who are exactly alike psychologically are exactly alike justificationally.[18] The second, 'internalism about defeat', is the view that defeat strongly supervenes on the internal in that any two possible agents who are exactly alike psychologically are exactly alike in terms of defeat.

It is easy enough to see that the two are related. Internalism in epistemology entails internalism about defeat. After all, it is analytic that defeat negatively affects one's justification. But if so, then any two possible agents who are justificationally alike must be alike in terms of defeat. And from this it follows that if internalism in epistemology is true – that is, if any two agents are psychologically alike, then they are alike justificationally – then internalism about defeat is true – that is, if any two agents are psychologically alike, then they are alike in terms of defeat.

In the Introduction, I mentioned a distinction between types of defeat that remains controversial among epistemologists, that is, the distinction between internal and external defeat. Recall that in cases of external defeat the defeaters are not psychologically registered by the relevant believers. It is easy to see that if internalism about defeat is true, there can be no such thing as external defeat. After all, if there is such a thing as external defeat, then since external defeat isn't psychologically registered, it will be possible for there to be two agents who are exactly alike psychologically and yet differ in terms of defeat. In particular, it may be that one of them has an external defeater and the other one doesn't.

The central aim of this section is to mount a case against internalism about defeat. Since internalism in epistemology entails internalism about defeat, my case against internalism about defeat is by the same token a case against

---

[18] Note that my characterisation aligns with a specific form of internalism known as mentalism (Conee and Feldman 2004). The main alternative is accessibilism (BonJour 1980; Chisholm 1977). While each view has its own motivations, I am focusing here on mentalism because it can easily allow for knowledge and justified belief in unsophisticated agents such as small children and animals. For more on the internalism/externalism divide, see Kornblith (2001).

internalism in epistemology. To this end, I will argue that there is such a thing external defeat (Section 2.2). Once this argument is in place, the question of whether there is such a thing as external defeat should be considerably less controversial than it has been in recent literature. However, I do not want to rest the case against internalism entirely on a kind of case that might be thought to be controversial. For that reason, I will provide some independent reason for thinking that the correct epistemology of defeat must be externalist (Section 2.3).

3.2 External Defeat

In what follows, I will argue that the phenomenon of testimonial injustice provides excellent reason to think that external defeat exists. To be clear, I don't mean to suggest that cases of testimonial injustice are the only cases of external defeat. Rather, my point is that they are particularly well suited to make a case for the existence of external defeat. In a nutshell, the reason for this is that certain cases of testimonial injustice make for excellent examples of cases of internal defeat and, once it is clear why these cases work as cases of internal defeat, it is hard to deny that there are also other cases of testimonial injustice that are cases of external defeat.

Testimonial injustice is one of the most important topics in recent epistemology. It is a distinctively epistemic kind of injustice. More specifically, in paradigm cases of testimonial injustice a hearer doesn't give a speaker the credibility that they deserve as a result of systematic prejudice (Fricker 2007). To take a famous example, consider the case of a research team featuring a group of men who don't believe anything the female team members say, because they are sexists (Lackey 2018). Now suppose that this group of men carries out some experiments that strongly support the hypothesis that p and that they come to believe that p on this basis. Suppose, next, some of the women on the team discover a serious flaw with the experiment, which they point out to the group in question. Due to sexist bias, the men discount the women's testimony and continue in their beliefs ('the sexist scientists case').

This is a paradigm case of testimonial injustice. In discounting the women's testimony due to sexist bias, the men fail to give their female colleagues the credibility they are due because of systematic prejudice. At the same time, it is also a paradigm case of defeat. After the women's testimony about the flaw in the experiment, the men's belief that p is no longer justified.

Now, this case is a case of internal defeat. After all, while the men don't know, nor believe what the women told them, they do know that (q =) some of their female colleagues told them that there is a serious flaw with the experiment. And the fact that q is itself widely acknowledged as constituting a defeater for their belief that p. Since the men know that q, they know a fact that constitutes a defeater for their belief that p. In this way, we have a case of internal defeat involving testimonial injustice.

Crucially, once we allow for cases of internal defeat involving testimonial injustice, it is hard to deny that we must allow for cases of external defeat also. To see why, note that at the root of the cases of internal defeat is a bad epistemic disposition, in the case at hand a systematic identity prejudice against women. It is this disposition that explains why the sexist scientists don't take their female colleagues' testimony into consideration and hence, ultimately, why their justification for believing that p is defeated.

With these points in play, we can now see why the route to external defeat is a short one. To begin with, let's consider a variation of the case in which the male scientists are radicalised in the following way. Not only do they have the disposition to dismiss testimony by women because of systematic identity prejudice, but they also think that what women have to say is simply not worth listening to in the first place. They are disposed to simply tune out whenever a female team member tells them something with the result that there isn't even uptake of what they were told in the first place. Otherwise put, in the original version of the case, the scientists continue to keep track of what their female colleagues say (but then go on to discount it). In the new version, they don't even keep track of what they say ('the radicalised sexist scientists case').

Now, here is one crucial point. It cannot be that now that the sexist scientists have become radicalised (in that their bad epistemic disposition has gotten worse because now they are not only disposed to discount the testimony of their female colleagues, but they are also disposed to not even listen to them), they have successfully insulated themselves from defeat they would have had had they been less radicalised (in that they are only disposed to discount the word of their female colleagues, but still listen to them). As a result, if the original version of the case is a case of defeat, then so is the new version. But since we have already seen that the original version is indeed a case of defeat, we have excellent reason to think that the same goes for the new version.

Here is another crucial point. The case of the radicalised sexist scientists is a case of external defeat. This is because, thanks to their radicalisation, none of the defeaters, that is, that the experiment is flawed or that the female colleagues asserted that it is flawed, is psychologically registered by the sexist scientists here. In this way, the phenomenon of testimonial injustice does provide a compelling reason to think that there is external defeat.

Before moving on, note that we do not need to appeal to distinctively testimonial cases to make this point. In fact, it is easy to see that we can construct similar cases that don't involve testimony as a source of belief. For instance, consider a case in which a teacher is asking a question to their class. The only student who raises their hand is black. Even though the entire class, including the black student, is in plain view, because of racist bias, the teacher simply doesn't register that the black student raised their hand. They form the belief that no one in the class is willing to answer the question and proceed to explaining the answer themselves ('the racist teacher case'). It is hard to deny that if the case of the radicalised sexist scientists is a case of external defeat, then so is the case of the racist teacher.

Cases like the radicalised sexist scientists and the racist teacher provide excellent reason for thinking that we need to make room in our epistemology for external defeat.[19] I have already provided reason to think that this is bad news for internalism about defeat, and, since internalism in epistemology entails internalism about defeat, for internalism in epistemology.

Might internalists resist this result and if so, how? One possible route is to insist that cases like the radicalised sexist scientists involve moral rather than epistemic failures. I don't find this move attractive. Here is why. First, it has the unpalatable consequence that tuning up epistemically bad properties can lead to an improvement of an agent's epistemic position. In the above case, making the sexist scientists more sexist such that they not only discount their female colleagues' testimony but also don't even tune in to what they say will amount to an improvement in their overall epistemic position. Second, consider yet another variation of the case in which the sexist scientists systematically mishear what they are told by female colleagues about their work. Whenever they encounter disagreement, they hear agreement. It is perhaps even harder to believe that this trait should lead to an improvement of their epistemic position towards the propositions in question. Third, note that we can now even drop the

---

[19] There are further arguments for the existence of external defeat. One is inspired by Mona Simion's (2023) argument that moral blameworthiness requires the absence of (epistemically) blameless ignorance. If so, in cases of moral blameworthiness, offenders are either aware that they are doing something wrong or else they (epistemically) should be. For instance, suppose one of the sexist scientists, A, is also the line manager of his female colleague, B, and that A promotes a male colleague, C, over B because of sexism. Suppose further that A isn't aware that he is doing something wrong. He thinks C deserves the promotion over B. But that's because, due to sexism, he pays close attention to C's work and not to B's. Now, we surely want to allow that A is morally blameworthy for his sexist promotion of C over B. But if so, since A is ignorant that it is wrong to promote C over B, we must allow that A falls short epistemically in that he should be aware that it is wrong to promote C over B but he isn't. However, it is hard to see how this could be unless we allow for external defeat.

Another argument is by Goldberg (2018) who adduces cases of agents occupying certain social roles. While I agree with Goldberg, I believe that his cases require a slightly different treatment than the one I am discussing here. Due to limitations of space, I will leave discussion of them for another occasion (Kelp and Simion 2023).

injustice component of the case. We may suppose that the scientists simply mistake disagreement *by anyone* for agreement. Again, it's implausible that, as a result, the scientists should be insulated from defeat. At the same time, the charge that the failure is really a moral one becomes less credible once the injustice component is removed. Finally, we can imagine that disaster will strike unless the scientists mistake disagreement for agreement – perhaps humanity stands to be wiped out entirely (e.g. by a capricious demon). In this case, it's morally best/permissible for the scientists to have an epistemically bad disposition. But this fact is orthogonal to the epistemic assessment of the case, which remains unchanged.

Another way to resist the above result is by insisting on a distinctively internalist version of evidentialism, according to which (i) one's justificatory status strongly supervenes on what evidence one has and (ii) the distinctively internalist thesis that what evidence one has strongly supervenes on the internal.[20] Internalist evidentialists might continue to insist that there is a key difference in the evidence the sexist scientists have in the original version of the case and in the new version of it. In particular, in the sexist scientists case, a defeater for p is part of their evidence, whereas in the radicalised sexist scientists case, it isn't. Evidentialism thus provides a reason for thinking that the two cases can be treated differently.

In my view, these considerations provide reason to think that internalist evidentialism is false as well. This is because the point remains that, in the case of the sexist scientists, radicalisation cannot lead to successful insulation from defeat. This is a point that any successful epistemology, evidentialism included, should accommodate. Since internalist evidentialism cannot do so, so much the worse for this view.[21]

Now, internalists will likely disagree here. Rather than continuing this line of argument, I want to change gear and argue that we don't need to appeal to distinctively external defeat to get internalism into trouble. Even ordinary cases of defeat will do the trick. The case against internalism about defeat (and hence against internalism in epistemology) can be made on independent grounds.

---

[20] Note that this version of evidentialism entails internalism in epistemology.

[21] Note that many externalists endorse a version of evidentialism that faces this problem. This is because while they deny that what evidence one has strongly supervenes on the internal, they endorse the claim that possession of evidence requires one to have psychologically registered it. It is easy to see that externalist evidentialists of this stripe will not be able to make sense of external defeat. In my view, that's a strike against these versions of externalist evidentialism, one they suffer because they are insufficiently externalist about what it takes to possess evidence. Note also that there are externalist versions of evidentialism that avoid this problem (e.g. Simion 2023).

3.3 Defeat Defeat

I'd like to begin with what may appear to be a slight detour. However, its relevance will become clear in due course. Consider three cases in which someone is driving their car. In all three cases, the driver believes that their child is in the back seat and needs urgent medical attention. Because of this, the driver breaks several traffic norms: they drive faster than permitted by local speed limits, they drive through red lights, and so on. Now, here is how the three cases come apart: in the first, the driver, A, knows that their child needs urgent medical attention; in the second, the driver, B, falsely believes this because of brainwashing. In the third, the driver, C, falsely believes this because they decided it would be fun to take a new drug and now C is hallucinating their child's injury.

Now consider the following question: do these drivers justifiably break the traffic norms in these cases? Fortunately, this question has an easy answer. This is because the three cases instantiate three familiar normative categories: in the first, A justifiably breaks the traffic norms; in the second, B does not justifiably break the traffic norms, but they are blameless for breaking them; in the third, C does not justifiably break the traffic norms and they are blameworthy for breaking them (albeit perhaps only indirectly[22] in virtue of being blameworthy for taking the drug).

Consider next epistemic analogues of these cases. In all three cases, the protagonists believe that they are a doctor at the local hospital and that they have just received notice to perform an emergency surgery in OR1. While they are preparing for surgery someone tells them that they are not a doctor and asks them to step away from the patient. Finally, the protagonists – X, Y, and Z – believe the testifier to be a notorious drug abuser and disruptive element in the hospital. In light of this belief, the three protagonists dismiss the testimony and hold on to their beliefs that they are a doctor. Here is how the three cases differ: in the first, X, knows that they are a doctor, and they know that the testifier is a notorious drug abuser and disruptive element; in the second, Y, does so because they falsely believe this due to brainwashing. In the third, Z, does so because they falsely believe this because they decided it would be fun to take a new drug which caused them to have a range of beliefs, including the false belief that they are a doctor and the false belief that the testifier is a drug abuser (in fact, the testifier is a doctor at the hospital).

Note that in all three cases, the testifier's testimony that the protagonists aren't doctors provides them with a defeater for their beliefs that they are doctors. This defeater is subsequently dismissed by the protagonists. With this

---

[22] For more on indirect blameworthiness see, for example, Zimmermann (1997).

point in play, I'd like to ask whether the protagonists justifiably dismiss this defeater. The answer here is no more difficult than in the driving cases. Again, the cases instantiate the familiar normative categories: X justifiably dismisses the defeater; Y does not justifiably dismiss the defeater, but they are blameless in doing so; Z does not justifiably dismiss the defeater, and they are blameworthy in doing so.

Crucially, note that we may assume that X, Y and Z are psychological duplicates and thus exactly alike psychologically. If so, internalism in epistemology is in trouble. This is because X, on the one hand, and Y and Z on the other are not exactly alike justificationally. After all, X justifiably dismisses the defeater at issue here, whereas Y and Z don't.[23]

What about internalism about defeat? Is this view in trouble as well? To answer this question, I'd first like to take a closer look at another distinction between the case of X on the one hand and the cases of Y and Z on the other. In the case of X, in which the defeater is justifiably dismissed, the defeater X has ends up being defeated itself. In other words, the case of X is not only a case of defeat, but also a case of defeat defeat. In contrast, in the cases of Y and Z, in which the defeater isn't justifiably dismissed, the defeaters Y and Z have end up not being defeated themselves. In other words, the cases of Y and Z are cases of defeat, but not cases of defeat defeat. But, of course, if this is correct, internalism about defeat is in trouble also. After all, since X, Y, and Z are exactly alike psychologically, they must be exactly alike in terms of defeat. As a result, internalism about defeat cannot allow that the case of X is a case of defeat defeat, while the cases of Y and Z are cases of defeat without defeat defeat.

What comes to light then is that there is reason to think that internalism about defeat (and hence internalism in epistemology) is false on independent grounds. We do not need to invoke cases of external defeat to show that internalism about defeat runs into trouble.

3.4 Conclusion

This section has mounted a case against internalism about defeat. More specifically, I have developed two arguments against this view.

First, I have provided reason to think that any adequate epistemology of defeat must allow for the existence of external defeat. Since internalism about defeat is incompatible with the existence of external defeat, there is reason to think that this view is false.

---

[23] Note that it won't help to relativise justification to distinctively epistemic justification. After all, X is epistemically justified in dismissing the defeater.

Since the existence of external defeat has been controversial amongst epistemologists, I have developed an alternative argument that appeals to cases of defeat defeat. The key idea here was that, in general, external properties matter to whether we break certain norms justifiably. Epistemology makes no exception. In particular, external properties of belief matter to whether we justifiably break norms of what to do in the face of defeat. But, of course, this is not something that internalists can allow. In this way, there is independent reason to think that internalism is false.

Finally, it may be worth noting that the second argument not only provides an alternative to the first, but it also helps it. After all, the fact that external defeat has remained controversial in epistemology is mainly because internalism is incompatible with the existence of external defeat. Once we see that internalism isn't an option, and especially once it is clear that internalism isn't an option in the epistemology of defeat, resistance to recognising the reality of external defeat may be expected to wane.

4 Externalism and Defeat

4.1 Introduction

We have seen that sceptical and internalist approaches to defeat are bound to remain unsuccessful. If so, then the correct epistemology of defeat must be externalist. Accordingly, this section will focus on extant externalist accounts of defeat.

Recall that one of the central reasons why internalist accounts of defeat fail is that we need to make room in our epistemology for external defeat. One of the main benefits of abandoning internalism in favour of externalism is that externalism can allow for external defeat, at least in principle.

At the same time, there is no shortage of externalist epistemologies that do not make room for external defeat in practice. This is because they embrace a limited form of internalism about defeat possession. In a nutshell, the idea is that to have a defeater one must either have some form of psychological relation to the defeater (e.g. Plantinga 2000), or one must be able to access the defeater from some internal state (e.g. Beddor 2021; Graham and Lyons 2021). It is easy enough to see that this means that these views foreclose the possibility of allowing for external defeat. After all, the very point of cases of external defeat is that agents who have them neither bear a psychological relation to them, nor can they access the defeaters from some internal state. But since we need to make room in our epistemology for external defeat, closing the door to an epistemology that allows for external defeat is a mistake. Accordingly, I will rest content with the observation that whatever else the merits of externalist epistemologies that don't allow for external defeat, there is room for improvement. If I succeed in developing a viable account of defeat that can successfully accommodate external defeat, then that's a reason to favour it over these views.

While some externalist accounts of defeat don't allow for external defeat, others do venture to do so. Since the account I will develop in due course cannot improve on these accounts simply by accommodating the existence of external defeat, I will take a closer look at each of these proposals in what follows.

4.2 Goldman

One of the most influential externalist accounts of defeat is Alvin Goldman's (e.g. 1979, 2012) alternative reliable process view. Goldman famously defends process reliabilism. Very roughly, according to process reliabilism, believing justifiably is a matter of believing via reliable processes. For a belief to have prima facie justification, again roughly, it must be produced via a reliable process. This leaves the question as to how to incorporate defeat into the picture. This is where the alternative reliable process view comes in. The key idea here is that of an alternative reliable process available to one such that, if it were used in addition to or instead of the process actually used, the relevant belief would not be produced in the agent. For instance, suppose I have a belief that the animal in the pen before me is a zebra, which was produced by a reliable perceptual process. According to process reliabilism, this belief is prima facie justified. Now suppose that you tell me that pen is populated by cleverly disguised mules. This is of course a familiar case of defeat. The way in which Goldman accounts for this is that I have an alternative reliable process, roughly, believing your testimony, such that were it used in addition to or instead of my perceptual process, I would not believe that the animal is a zebra. That's how the justification for my belief is defeated.

It is easy enough to see that the alternative reliable process view does not close the door to external defeat. After all, it may be that in cases of external defeat the agents have the right kind of alternative reliable process available to them. For instance, in the radicalised sexist scientists case, it may be that the process of believing what their female colleagues told them is a process that is available to them. Whether it is will turn on what it takes for a process to be available. Unfortunately, Goldman does not offer a detailed account here. What's more, what he does say suggests that he may be siding with limited internalists here: 'What I think we should have in mind here are such additional processes as calling previously acquired evidence to mind, assessing the implications of that evidence, etc. (Goldman 1979, 20).'

This looks very much like Goldman is thinking of available processes as processes that take internal states as inputs. That said, even if Goldman thinks that we should have in mind processes that take internal states as inputs, it remains open whether he would in the end agree that we should only have these processes in mind. If the answer here is no, then the door to external defeat remains open.

At this stage, we may try to explore whether there is an account of what it takes for a process to be available that does the trick for the alternative reliable process view. However, I will not go down that route here. This is because the view fails on independent grounds: defeat comes out as insufficiently norma-tive, as it were. This point is forcefully made by Bob Beddor (2015), who argues that the fact that you may have a sceptic-emulating process available that, were it to be used in addition to or instead of any belief-forming process you may use, would lead to you not having any belief at all does not mean that the justification for all of your beliefs is defeated. And the reason for this is that, even though you *would* not have believed had you used this alternative process, it's not the case that you *should* not have believed, because it is not the case that you should have used this alternative process.

In this way, it ultimately doesn't matter whether champions of the alternative reliable process view can develop an account of what it takes for alternative processes to be available that accommodates external defeat: there is reason to think that the view fails on independent grounds.

4.3 Sosa

Ernest Sosa (e.g. 2015, 2021) is a virtue epistemologist who has a very elaborate epistemology, with a true wealth of normative categories. For present purposes, I will not venture to offer anything close to a full account of his view. Instead, I will focus on a couple of key ideas that will allow me to get the points about defeat I want to make into focus. The first is that the central object of epistemic evaluation are judgements. The second is that whether a judgement is justified turns on whether it is competent.

Now, Sosa does not develop an account of defeat for his virtue epistemology. However, his recent work prominently features negligence. Most importantly for present purposes, according to Sosa, negligence may undermine compe-tence (2021, 63). Since Sosa analyses justification in terms of competence, the result that we get is that negligence can undermine justification. In this way, on Sosa's view, negligence is a route to defeat. More specifically, there is reason to think that a viable account of negligence will allow us to make progress towards an account of external defeat. After all, cases of external defeat can plausibly be viewed as cases of negligence. For instance, the radicalised sexist scientists behave negligently when they don't even listen to what their female colleagues tell them. In this way, the prospects of an account of external defeat in terms of negligence are starting to look up.

Of course, key here will be a viable account of negligence. And while Sosa does not deliver a full account, he does develop the beginnings of one. He considers a case in which you are adding numbers via mental arithmetic. If the set of numbers you are adding is sufficiently large, you will not be sufficiently reliable to arrive at a competent judgement about the sum. Suppose you are still sufficiently reliable but barely so. At the same time, you have a calculator ready at hand, which would keep you safely above the relevant threshold. If you insist on mental arithmetic here, Sosa argues, you fall foul of negligence (2021, 63).

Sosa's key theoretical idea is that if you can assess your first order competence by more reliable means but fail to do so, then you are negligent. In particular, you fall foul of a kind of negligence that precludes what he calls the competent attainment of aptness. Most importantly for present purposes, given that competent judgement requires competent attainment of apt belief, it precludes competent judgement.

While this does offer the beginning of a substantive account of negligence and so brings the prospects of a workable account of external defeat in terms of negligence into view, there is reason to think that this account remains ultimately unsatisfactory. More specifically, it is too strong. To see this, consider a case in which I ask my flatmate whether we have milk left. They tell me that we do. Now, I do have several more reliable means available to me of assessing my first order competence. For instance, I could also ask my other flatmate, or I could open the fridge and look for myself. Crucially, however, failure to avail myself of these means doesn't make me negligent. And, most importantly for present purposes, it doesn't preclude my judgement that there is milk in the fridge from being competent.

It may be worth reflecting on why Sosa's account fails: just like the alternative reliable process view, Sosa's account is insufficiently normative. According to the kind of view we are considering, cases of external defeat involve the availability of alternative means that would lead to a more reliable assessment of first order aptness and competence. Crucially, *pace* Sosa, what matters is not (only) whether one has alternative means *available* that would lead one to a more reliable assessment of first order aptness and competence, but (also) whether one *should* have availed oneself of these means. In the case of the radicalised sexist scientists, they should have listened to their female colleagues. In the milk case, it is not the case that I should have had a look myself or asked someone else in addition.

4.4 Goldberg

Sanford Goldberg's (2018) account of defeat centrally involves social roles. One key thought is that social roles come with normative expectations. These normative expectations may and often enough are epistemic. Another key thought is that to believe that p justifiably one must live up to these expectations. With these points in play, we can already see how Goldberg may want to account for cases of external defeat. In the radicalised sexist scientists case, for instance, the sexist scientists are part of a team of researchers. In this way, they occupy a social role. By the first key thought, they are subject to normative expectations that are associated with this social role. In particular, they are subject to the expectation to listen to what other team members tell them about their research. Since they don't live up to this expectation, by the second key thought, they do not believe that p justifiably.

One worry that immediately arises is about the relation between social epistemic expectations and epistemic norms. Note that if epistemic norms have explanatory priority over epistemic expectations, we will not make much headway towards a viable account of external defeat. After all, it is precisely these epistemic norms that we need to explain if we are to give a satisfactory account of external defeat. Crucially, this worry can be laid to rest quickly. The reason for this is that Goldberg develops a view that reverses the standard direction of explanation between norms and expectations. According to Goldberg, epistemic norms are explained in terms of social epistemic expectations rather than the other way around (2018, 147).

If Goldberg is right and epistemic norms are grounded in social epistemic expectations, the question arises as to what, if anything, social epistemic expectations are grounded in. Goldberg's answer appeals to the fact that we are deeply social creatures who are engaged in practices of information sharing and joint action. These practices are supported by a rationale in that opting out of them would be practically irrational for us. Crucially, these practices can only be supported by this kind of rationale if we are entitled to certain expectations. In this way, the social epistemic expectations that ground epistemic norms are themselves grounded in the rationality of our practices of information sharing and joint action (2018, 153–7).

Goldberg's account is much more detailed than this. However, the structure of the account should be in clear enough view, at least to get my central worry into sharp relief. Most importantly, the key idea for present purposes is that epistemic normativity is ultimately grounded in the rationality of our practices of information-sharing and joint action. But if that is so, the scope of epistemic normativity only reaches as far as our rationale-supported practices of information-sharing and joint action. And the problem is that this is too limited.

Consider a society that has practices of sharing information and acting jointly on a wide range of issues. At the same time, this society also doesn't have a practice of sharing information and acting jointly on other issues. To take an example close to home, suppose that they don't have a practice of sharing information and acting jointly on cases of sexual abuse. What's more, victims are not to be helped in any way either. Since there is no practice of sharing information and engaging in joint action on this issue, there can be no social epistemic expectations here either, at least not if Goldberg is right and these expectations are grounded in our practices of sharing information and joint action. But if it is practice-generated expectations that explain epistemic normative standards, the result that we get is that whatever epistemic norm there may be that requires (or at least permits) members of this society to trust the word of others will not extend to the word of victims of sexual abuse. As a result, in this society the word of victims of sexual abuse cannot function as a defeater for beliefs in the innocence of sexual predators. And that, clearly, is the wrong result. It cannot be that we diminish the epistemic status of the testimony of victims of sexual abuse simply by tuning up the degree of sexism in a society.

The problem Goldberg encounters here is grounded in the absence of certain social practices. A perhaps even more dramatic version of the problem arises from the presence of bad social practices. Consider a community of agents that has a social practice of actively distrusting the testimony of victims of sexual abuse. This practice not only fails to give rise to epistemic expectations, but it also gives rise to bad epistemic expectations. For instance, one expectation this practice gives rise to is that those who claim to have suffered sexual abuse are liars. If it is practice-generated expectations that explain epistemic normative standards, the result that we threaten to end up with here is that the word of victims of sexual abuse can permissibly be disregarded (in other words, members of this community threaten to end up having standing defeaters for the word of victims of sexual abuse, simply as a result of having a bad social practice). And, of course, this result is even worse for Goldberg's account.

4.5 Simion

The last view I'd like to look at is due to Mona Simion (2023). Her key idea is that defeaters are indicators of ignorance. More precisely, q is a defeater for your evidence, e, that p if and only if you are in a position to know q and the probability of p given e and q is lower than the probability of p given e alone (Simion 2023, Section 2).

Key to making this account of defeat more precise is an account of what it takes to be in a position to know something. There are two key elements to this. First, one must have a cognitive process that has the function of generating knowledge. Second, this cognitive process must be able to easily take up p in cognisers of one's type. And, conversely, if one has a cognitive process that has the function of generating knowledge and that can easily take up p in cognisers of one's type, then one is in a position to know that p (2023, Section 2).

Finally, Simion fleshes out what it takes for a process to be able to easily take up something in terms of a set of limitations. More specifically, she distinguishes among qualitative, quantitative, and environmental limitations on easy uptake. Qualitative limitations have to do with whether a cogniser of one's type can process the type of information in question. Quantitative limitations have to do with whether a cogniser of one's type can process the amount of information in question. Environmental limitations have to do with whether a cogniser of one's type can find this information in their environment given the laws of nature and social norms (2023, Section 2).

Again, it is easy enough to see that Simion's account can accommodate external defeat. For instance, even though the radicalised sexist scientists don't listen to what their female colleagues tell them, they are in a position to know at the very least that their female colleagues told them that there is a problem with their experiment. After all, they have a cognitive process (standardly involved in the reception of testimony) that has the function of generating knowledge that a certain testifier just told them such and so. What's more, this process can easily take up the fact that their female colleagues just told them that there is a problem with their experiment. Most importantly, easy uptake is not impeded by any of the relevant limitations of quality, quantity, and environment.

Given that the sexist scientists are in a position to know that their female colleagues told them that there is a problem with their experiment, the question as to whether they have a defeater boils down to the question as to whether the probability of p given their experiment and the fact that their colleagues told them about the problem is lower than the probability of p given the experiment alone. Since it clearly is, the case is correctly classified as a case of defeat. Simion's account successfully makes room for external defeat.

As will become clear in due course, Simion's view is quite similar to my own in that my view also explains justification and defeat ultimately in terms of functions. The perhaps most important difference between the two views is that, on my view, justification and defeat are agent-relative: justification and defeat are explained in terms of abilities, where abilities involve processes that have the function of generating knowledge in the possessor of the ability. In contrast, Simion's view is agent-neutral: justification and defeat are explained in terms of processes that have the function of generating knowledge in cognisers of one's type.

The main reason why I prefer the agent-relative view has to do with the fact that the agent-neutral view allows for a version of a famous problem of accidental reliability (e.g. BonJour 1980; Lehrer 1990). To get the problem into view, consider Lehrer's (1990) famous case of Mr Truetemp who, unbeknownst to him, has been fitted with intracranial 'Truetemp' device that allows him to keep track of the temperature by producing spontaneous beliefs about the temperature whenever there is a change of at least one degree centigrade. The classical version of the case is famously used to argue against standard process reliabilism on the grounds that Mr Truetemp's belief-forming process is reliable but the beliefs it produces are not justified.

Now, knowledge first views of justification, which take knowledge rather than true belief to be the central epistemic value, can handle this case quite easily. After all, the beliefs Mr Truetemp forms are not only not justified, but they also fall short of knowledge. This means that while the process is reliable in the sense that it produces beliefs with a favourable truth to falsity ratio, it is not reliable in the sense that it produces beliefs with a favourable knowledge to ignorance ratio. On knowledge first views of justification, then Mr Truetemp's beliefs are not justified.

The trouble is that the problem resurfaces for views like Simion's. To see this, consider a version of the Truetemp case in which I am currently developing this device. You have agreed to test the product for me and have it fitted. Upon trying it out you notice that there are some problems, say, that the device is slightly inaccurate. I go back and work a bit more on it, then take it back to you and you give it another test run. Finally, the Truetemp device works perfectly, and you acquire knowledge about temperature with its help. Perhaps a number of people now have been fitted with the device with the result that the Truetemp device has the function of generating knowledge in normal adult human beings. Finally suppose that Mr Truetemp has no idea that this device exists and has it fitted completely unbeknownst to him. In that case, he is no better off than the original Mr Truetemp: the beliefs he now forms are not justified. However, they are produced by a belief-forming process that has the function of generating knowledge in agents of his type. So, Simion's view predicts that these beliefs are justified. Simion's agent-neutral view runs into trouble. In contrast, while the Truetemp device may have the function of generating knowledge in adult humans, it does not have the function of generating knowledge in Mr Truetemp. For that, Mr Truetemp would have to train up with the device in the way you did, or he would have to know that it works. In this way, the agent-relative view does better (Kelp 2023).

Of course, this problem concerns Simion's account of prima facie justification. However, it is easy to see that it will also cause trouble for her account of defeat. After all, on Simion's view, once fitted with the Truetemp device, Mr Truetemp has evidence that he must take into consideration when forming beliefs about the temperature. For instance, suppose Mr Truetemp looks at a thermometer which reads 22 degrees centigrade. If the reading conflicts with the indication by the

Truetemp device, he cannot justifiably believe that it is 22 degrees in the way he could had he not been fitted with the device. This is because the indication by the Truetemp device provides him with a defeater for this belief. However, that just doesn't seem right. On the contrary, if Mr Truetemp could just ignore the indication by the Truetemp device and form a belief based only on the reading of the thermometer, that's exactly what he should do.

4.6 Conclusion

This section has focused on externalist accounts of defeat. Several epistemologists have taken this challenge to motivate combining an externalist epistemology with an internalist account of defeat. Even so, once we realise that we must make room for external defeat in our epistemology, the prospects for this kind of view look less and less bright. Accordingly, I have focused on externalist epistemologies that can offer a more sanguine approach to external defeat.

More specifically, I looked at two approaches that may accommodate external defeat by appealing to available alternative processes (Goldman) or means (Sosa). Both of these remain ultimately unsuccessful because they are insufficiently normative.

Another option, due to Goldberg, ventures to account for external defeat in terms of social epistemic expectations, which, in turn, are grounded in the rationality of our information sharing and joint action practices. The problem here is that these practices may be quite limited, or they may even be bad. And when the practices that ultimately ground epistemic norms are too limited or bad, the norms that we get will undergenerate defeat.

The last option is by Simion who offers a functionalist account of defeat. While the view that I will develop in due course is quite similar to Simion's, the two diverge on at least one important count. According to Simion's view, the functions that explain defeat are agent neutral, while according to my view, they are agent relative. I have provided reason to think that, as a result of agent-neutrality, Simion runs into trouble with Truetemp cases. Unsurprisingly, these problems generate further problems with defeat.

In sum, while there are a few promising externalist accounts of defeat on the market, there is reason to think that none of them are ultimately viable.

5 Virtue Epistemology and Internal Defeat

5.1 Introduction

The remainder of this Element develops a viable account of defeat. More specifically, this section will focus on internal defeat and the next one will turn to external defeat. Here is the game plan for this section. Section 4.2 introduces virtue epistemology, which is the epistemological theory for which I develop an account of defeat. It also raises a problem that accounts like this are unable to accommodate the phenomenon of defeat altogether. Section 4.3 develops a solution to this problem. In Section 4.4, I develop the backbone of a more substantive account of defeat and show how it can handle paradigm cases of internal defeat.

5.2 Virtue Epistemology

I'd like to start by saying a few words about virtue epistemology. Virtue epistemology is associated with a normative framework that allows us to assess attempts with constitutive aims such as archery shots and basketball free throws. (Following (Sosa 2021) I will henceforth also refer to this framework as 'telic normativity'.) Since attempts have constitutive aims, we can ask whether or not a given attempt is *successful*. Most importantly for present purposes, we can also ask whether a given attempt is *competent*, that is, produced by an ability to attain the attempt's aim. Finally, we can ask whether a given attempt is *apt*, that is, successful because competent.

Now, virtue epistemologists standardly take beliefs to be attempts that have truth as their constitutive aims. That said, my own preferred view is that belief constitutively aims at knowledge rather than truth (Kelp 2021a, 2021b). While I will leave the question as to who is right on this issue open for now, I will return to it in due course. Given that belief is a kind of attempt, telic normativity applies to belief. We can ask whether beliefs are successful, that is, whether they are true/knowledge. In addition, we can also ask whether they are competent, that is, whether they are produced by an ability to believe truly/know. And, finally, we can ask whether they are apt, that is, successful because competent.

Virtue epistemology identifies epistemic properties such as justified belief and knowledge with properties of telic normativity. In particular, knowledge is identified with apt belief[24] and, most importantly for present purposes, justified belief is identified with competent belief.[25] This is the account that I will develop an epistemology of defeat for.

As a first observation, there is reason for optimism about an account of defeat for this kind of view. This is because there is excellent reason to think that defeat can undermine competence of attempts more generally. Suppose that you are about to take a shot in archery. As you aim for the bullseye, I tell you that there is

---

[24] On a knowledge-centric version of virtue epistemology, success and aptness coincide in the case of belief, that is, a belief is apt if and only if it is successful. See Kelp (2017, 2018) for an argument that this is not a problematic consequence of the view.

[25] For more on virtue epistemology see Fernández Vargas (2016); Greco and Turri (2013); Kelp and Greco (2020).

a strong wind blowing from the right ('the archery case'). In this case, you need to adjust your aim to shoot competently. If you aim for the bullseye in exactly the same way you would were there to be no wind, your shot won't be competent. It is plausible enough to think that when you take a shot that is aimed right at the bullseye here, your shot is not competent because it is subject to defeat. In particular, it is plausible enough that my testimony that there is a wind blowing from the right constitutes a defeater for your shot, at least if it is aimed right at the bullseye. But, of course, if there is reason to think that defeat can undermine competence of attempts in general, there is reason to think that it can do so in the particular epistemic case we are interested in. This means that it should be possible to give an account of defeat for virtue epistemology.

At the same time, incorporating a viable account of defeat into virtue epistemology is by no means a trivial task. To see this, note that beliefs for which we have defeaters may be produced by epistemic abilities. Suppose you tell me that the pen before me of is populated predominantly by cleverly disguised mules. I nonetheless form a perceptual belief that the animal I am looking at is a zebra ('the zebra case'). My belief will be the product of an exercise of an epistemic ability to tell a zebra from the way it looks. If this isn't obvious, note that had there not been cleverly disguised mules around, my belief would have qualified as knowledge.[26] As a result, it is hard to deny that my belief was produced by the exercise of an epistemic ability. After all, if it hadn't been produced by such an exercise, it is hard to see why it would have qualified as knowledge had there not been cleverly disguised mules around. In this way, there is reason to think that beliefs for which we have defeaters may be produced by epistemic abilities.[27]

What's more, the problem arises for attempts for which we have defeaters more generally. Suppose, in the archery case, I am about to take a shot and you tell me that the there is a wind blowing from the right. Suppose I nonetheless take a shot that is aimed right at the bullseye. My shot will be the product of an exercise of my ability to hit the target. Once again, this is evidenced by the fact that had there not been a wind blowing, my shot would have found the bullseye. In this way, there is reason to believe that you can also exercise your ability to hit the target no matter whether you have also learned that there is wind blowing from the right.

We saw earlier on that there is reason to think that defeat can undermine competence of attempts. At the same time, it transpires that attempts for which we have defeaters can be produced by relevant abilities, both in epistemic and non-epistemic cases. In this way, we are already in serious trouble. The virtue

---

[26] I am assuming (as I may) that had there not been cleverly disguised mules around, you wouldn't have told me that there are.

[27] This is another instance of the problem that we encountered in Lasonen-Aarnio's discussion of safety accounts of knowledge in Section 1.

epistemological view doesn't appear have the resources to accommodate the idea that defeat can undermine the competence of attempts.[28]

5.3 The Structure of Defeat: Defeaters as Range-Shifting

Thinking about defeat quickly leads to difficulties for the virtue epistemological view. Fortunately, there is a solution to this problem, which I will develop in what follows.

First, note that there is independent reason to think that competence of attempts requires more than merely being produced by an exercise of an ability to attain the relevant success. To see this, consider the following case. You are a basketball player who has the ability to make layups. The game you are currently playing is about to end. You only have two seconds to score a basket to win the game from your midcourt position. Suppose that you produce a shot via an exercise of your ability to make layups, which, of course, doesn't even get the ball close to the basket (Kelp 2017, 2018, 2019).

In this case your shot is not competent. At the same time, it is produced via the exercise of an ability to score baskets. This means that a competent attempt requires more than being produced by the exercise of an ability to succeed. What more? One very plausible thought is that a competent attempt needs to be produced by an exercise of the *right kind* of ability. In the above case, your ability to produce layups isn't the right kind of ability for what you are attempting to do, that is, score a basket from midcourt.

This raises the question as to what it takes for an attempt to be produced by the right kind of ability. To answer it, note that it is independently plausible that abilities are relative to ranges of attempt types. For instance, your ability to score layups in basketball is relative to a range of types of attempts you may make. It extends to attempts to score baskets from some distances but not others, it may extend to attempts to score baskets from some angles and not others, and so on. Crucially, shots from midcourt aren't in the range of your ability to score layups. Accordingly, here is how the point that abilities are relative to ranges of attempt types can give us

---

[28] One might wonder whether this isn't too quick. After all, virtue epistemologists standardly take abilities to be relative to conditions, C. And couldn't they just hold that defeat undermines competence by precluding C? No. While abilities are relative to C, virtue epistemologists will do well not to take competent attempts to require that C be in place. Consider a case in which you take a shot that would have hit the target had it not been for a gust of wind that no one could have predicted. In this case, your shot is clearly competent. If we take competent attempts to require that C obtain, we cannot accommodate this datum. After all, your ability to hit the target is relative to sufficiently normal winds. This point is, if anything, even more important when we turn to the envisaged applications in epistemology. After all, there is a range of cases in which C are not satisfied and yet agents form justified beliefs. Gettier cases and sceptical cases are the most prominent examples here. To secure the correct verdict that agents in Gettier and sceptical cases have justified beliefs, it is imperative that virtue epistemologists allow that attempts can be competent even when C are not in place.

an attractive way of unpacking what it takes for an attempt to be produced by the right kind of ability: the attempt must be in the range of the ability that produced it. The view of competent attempts that we get is one on which a competent attempt requires not only that it is produced via an exercise of a relevant ability but also that the attempt is in the range of the ability exercised. On this view, then, the reason why your shot from midcourt is not competent when it is produced via an exercise of an ability to score layups is that midcourt shots aren't in the range of the ability to score layups (Kelp 2017, 2018, 2019).

With these points in play, let's return to the case of defeat of competence. Recall that here I tell you that there is a wind blowing from the right. When you go on to take a shot that is aimed right at the bullseye, your shot is not competent. In particular, your knowledge of what I told you constitutes a defeater here. Now, the crucial point is that once you know that there is a wind blowing from the right, the ability that involves aiming straight at the bullseye isn't the right kind of ability for what you are attempting, that is, hitting the target while a wind is blowing from the right. In this respect, the problem here is the same as in the above basketball case.

We are now in a position to see how a view that takes abilities to be relative to ranges of attempt types can accommodate the idea of defeat undermining competence of attempts in general and belief in particular. It does so by shifting the range of the abilities at issue. For instance, in the archery case, coming to know what I tell you shifts the range of your ability to hit the target by aiming right at the bullseye with the result that if you take a shot via the exercise of this ability, your shot will not be competent. Similarly, in the zebra case, coming to know that most of the animals in the pen before you are cleverly disguised mules shifts the range of your ability to acquire true beliefs/knowledge about the presence of zebras. In particular, if you now come to believe that the animal is a zebra by standard perceptual means, your belief will not be competent. In fact, in both cases, your range-shifting knowledge constitutes a defeater which makes your attempt fall short of being competent.

5.4 The Substance of Defeat: Defeaters as Evidence for Unsuccessful Attempts

The account of defeaters as range shifters allows us fit defeaters within the virtue epistemological framework. While this allows us to understand what defeaters are structurally within virtue epistemology, the question of a more substantive account of defeat remains open. If this isn't immediately obvious, let's return to the zebra case once more. Recall that you come to know that the pen before you is mostly populated by cleverly disguised mules. This constitutes a defeater for your belief that the animal you are looking at is a zebra. What we can say now is that your knowledge about the cleverly disguised mules shifts the range of your ability to come to know that the animal is a zebra by looking. However, the question as to why exactly it is that this knowledge constitutes a defeater – that is, why exactly it is that it shifts the range of your ability – remains open. In what follows, I will begin to answer it by developing a more substantive account of defeat.

Recall the lightweight characterisation of defeat as involving reasons against holding certain beliefs. What's more, we saw that there is reason to think that defeaters can undermine competence of attempts more generally. Given that this is so, it's plausible to generalise the lightweight characterisation in the following way: defeaters involve reasons against attempting; or, at the very least, they are reasons against attempting in a certain way.

It is worth noting that, on the virtue epistemological picture that emerges, not every reason against attempting (in a certain way) is competence-undermining. Suppose I offer you a considerable sum of money for not aiming your next arrow right at the bullseye. Now, you have a reason against attempting in a certain way. However, this doesn't mean that you have a competence-undermining reason for not aiming your next shot at the bullseye. If this isn't obvious, note that while taking a shot aimed right at the bullseye may well be practically irrational, it doesn't mean that a shot thus aimed is not competent.

Again, something similar may be said of the epistemic case. If you offer me a considerable sum of money for not believing that there is a laptop before me, I may have a reason against believing that there is a laptop before me. However, this doesn't mean that I have a justification-undermining reason for my perceptual belief that there is indeed a laptop before more. Even if forming this belief is now practically irrational, it doesn't mean that my perceptual belief isn't justified.[29]

What comes to light is that not all reasons against attempting are competence-undermining. This may be because not all such reasons are defeaters or because not all defeaters undermine competence, at least by the lights of virtue epistemology. I do not mean to settle this question here. Instead, I will rest content with noting that since, on the present view, it is competence-undermining reasons against attempting that are of distinctive epistemological interest, it is competence-undermining reasons that I will focus on in what follows and that I will refer by 'defeaters'.

But what distinguishes defeaters from reasons against attempting that aren't competence-undermining? Here is my suggestion. *Defeaters are evidence that*

---

[29] Some think that there cannot be practical reasons against believing (e.g. Shah 2006). It is possible to run a version of the case with what, on the face of it, is a kind of epistemic reason: you are offered a trove of knowledge in exchange for not believing. If you think that in this case there isn't a reason against believing either, what you think may entail that reasons against believing are defeaters in the epistemic case. Even so, since virtue epistemology's background normative framework extends beyond the epistemic case and since a similar move is not promising for attempts in general, the point remains worth bearing in mind.

attempting, or at least attempting in a certain way, isn't successful.[30] While a handsome sum of money or the promise of a trove of knowledge may constitute a reason against attempting, it does not constitute evidence that attempting (in a certain way) isn't successful. On the present view, it is not a defeater for shooting or believing in a certain way. At the same time, in the archery case, that a wind is blowing from the right is evidence that taking a shot aimed at the bullseye isn't successful. Likewise, in the zebra case, that the pen is populated predominantly by cleverly disguised mules is evidence that your perceptual belief that the animal before you is a zebra doesn't qualify as knowledge. These pieces of evidence are reasons that are competence-undermining and so defeaters for the attempts in question.

Now that we have a view of what defeaters are on the virtue epistemological account I am developing, let's move on to the question under what conditions defeaters actually do undermine some justification one has. To this end, recall the distinction between the psychological and the normative view from the Introduction. Recall, further, that I argued that if there is such a thing as external defeat, then the psychological view cannot be correct. Since we have now seen that there is reason to countenance external defeat, there is also reason to think that the psychological view cannot be correct. Crucially, the normative view differs from the psychological view in that it has the resources to deny the psychological view's claim that a psychological relation is necessary for a defeater to undermine justification. This is because what matters on the normative view is positive epistemic standing: for a defeater to undermine justification it must be epistemically proper for one to have it.[31] On the normative view that emerges, then, a defeater, d, undermines one's justification if and only if it is epistemically proper for one to have d. And, more generally, a defeater, d, undermines the competence of an attempt if and only if it is epistemically proper for one to have d.

With these points in play, let's take a look at how the virtue epistemological view of defeat handles paradigm cases of defeat. In the archery case, you acquire testimonial knowledge that there is a wind blowing from the right.

---

[30] Standard virtue epistemologists who take belief to constitutively aim at truth may opt for an account of competence-undermining reason against attempting in terms of aptness rather than truth. Since on my view belief constitutively aims at knowledge, and since, in any case, aptness and success coincide in the case of belief, I will set this complication aside here.

[31] I take 'epistemically proper' to denote a generic normative property, signalling the existence of some corresponding epistemic norm. It is meant to remain neutral on what specific type of epistemic norm we are dealing with here. For instance, it is meant to remain neutral on whether the norm has the force of a 'should', a 'may', or something else entirely. As I will argue in due course, I take the relevant norms to be generated by functions (Section 5.3). Accordingly, for present purpose, I will rest content with observing that the further question about the nature of the norm under consideration will be settled by whatever the correct theory of the normative import of functions says about this.

Since you epistemically properly have defeaters that you know to be true, since it is epistemically proper for you to have defeaters that you epistemically properly have, it follows that it is epistemically proper for you to have defeaters that you know to be true. Moreover, since the fact that there is a wind blowing from the right is a defeater for your attempt to hit the target by aiming straight at the bullseye, if you do aim your shot right at the bullseye, your shot will not be competent. Likewise, in the zebra case, when the zookeeper tells you that the pen before you is mostly populated by cleverly disguised mules, you come to know what you are told. In addition, that the zookeeper tells you about the presence of cleverly disguised mules is a defeater for your belief that the animal you are looking at is a zebra. As a result, if you hold on to this belief, your belief will not be competent/justified.

What about cases of misleading defeat? For instance, consider a version of the archery case ('the misleading archery case') in which the person telling you that there is a wind blowing from the right is feeding you misinformation. In fact, there is no wind at all. Or consider a version of the zebra case ('the misleading zebra case') in which what the zookeeper tells you is false. In fact, there are no cleverly disguised mules in the pen.

Now, I want to allow that cases of misleading defeat are genuine cases of defeat. Accordingly, the cases behave in much the same way as cases of non-misleading defeat. Of course, there is one important difference. In cases of misleading defeat, you cannot acquire certain pieces of knowledge. For instance, in the misleading zebra case, you cannot come to know that the pen before you is mostly populated by cleverly disguised. Accordingly, we cannot explain how your belief that the animal before you is a zebra is defeated in quite the same way. And the same goes, mutatis mutandis, for the misleading archery case.

Fortunately, this is not much of a problem. There are at least two alternative ways of explaining how defeat occurs in these cases. One is that while knowledge of defeaters is sufficient for epistemically properly having defeaters, it's not necessary. In fact, justified belief is sufficient as well. Since, in cases of misleading defeat, even if you don't know the defeaters to be true, you justifiably believe them to be true, we still get the result that you epistemically properly have them. And now the explanation of why your attempt is not competent can proceed in much the same way as in cases of non-misleading defeat. Alternatively, note that the fact on the ground isn't the only fact that provides a defeater for your attempt. For instance, in the zebra case, the fact that there are cleverly disguised mules in the pen isn't the only defeater for your belief that the animal before you is a zebra. Another defeater is the fact that you were told that the pen is mostly populated by cleverly disguised mules. And this fact is a fact that you can come to know even if you are in the misleading zebra case. And, again, the same goes, mutatis mutandis, for the misleading archery case. Accordingly, we can also explain why your attempts are not competent in terms of a defeater that you do know.

One might wonder what happens when, in a case of misleading defeat, one dismisses the defeater and goes ahead with the attempt anyway. For instance, in the misleading archery case, what happens when one disregards the testimony that there is a wind blowing from the right and takes a shot aimed straight at the bullseye? Similarly, what happens when one disregards the testimony about cleverly disguised mules and forms a belief that the animal before one is a zebra. The answer is that even if one's attempt is successful, it is not competent and hence not apt. Again, the key point is that cases of misleading defeat behave in exactly the same way as cases of non-misleading defeat.

But is that correct? Perhaps it is plausible in the epistemic case. Even if the defeater one acquires is misleading, it is still plausible that one loses justification for one's belief and that one's belief falls short of knowledge. However, is the same true in non-epistemic cases? Suppose you are about to take a shot in archery. You are told that there is a wind blowing from the right. Suppose this testimony is false. In fact, there is no wind blowing at all. At the same time, you have no reason to think so and every reason to think that the testimony that there is a wind blowing from the right is true. Even so, you disregard it, take a shot that is aimed straight at the bullseye which hits the target. Isn't your shot apt and therefore competent?

No. If this isn't immediately obvious, consider a variation of the case in which you are also told that there is a wind blowing from the right. What's more, it is also the case that this testimony is false. Crucially, unlike in the previous version, the reason why it is false is not that there is no wind at all. Rather, it is that there is a wind blowing from the left. Just like in the previous version, you disregard the testimony and take a shot that is aimed right at the bullseye, which misses by a long way. Of course, in this case, your shot isn't apt and so cannot be competent because apt. Is it competent then? Clearly not. But now note that the only difference between the two cases is in the environmental conditions (no wind vs. wind from the left). Crucially, according to virtue epistemology, competence of attempts isn't sensitive to differences in purely environmental conditions. As a result, there is reason to think that, in the original version of the misleading archery case, your shot is also not competent.[32]

---

[32] Here are some considerations that may help explain how those who are attracted to the claim that, in the misleading archery case, the archer's shot is apt and therefore competent may have fallen into error. First, the shot is successful and, indeed it is successful because of the exercise of ability. Since success because of the exercise of ability and aptness typically coincide, it is easy to mistake the former for the latter. Second, you may come to know that your shot was successful

5.5 Conclusion

This section has developed a novel account of defeat for virtue epistemology. I have developed an account of defeaters as evidence that attempting, or at least attempting in a certain way, is unsuccessful. In addition, I argued for an account of defeat that is normative in that a defeater defeats some justification one has when it is epistemically proper for one to have the defeater. I showed that this account can accommodate plausible cases in which defeat undermines competence of attempts both in epistemology and beyond.

6 Virtue Epistemology and External Defeat

6.1 Introduction

The previous section developed a virtue epistemological account of defeat. One key idea is that in cases of defeat, the ranges of the abilities required for justified belief shift. A second key idea is that defeaters are evidence that attempting, or at least attempting in a certain way, isn't successful. A third key idea is that defeaters undermine justification (by shifting ranges of abilities) if and only if it is epistemically proper for one to have them.

This section aims to show how the virtue epistemological view can accommodate external defeat. The first and the second key ideas of the view work in exactly the same way as for internal defeat. What will require special attention is the third key idea. In cases of internal defeat, what happens is that we know or justifiably believe the relevant defeaters. More generally, in cases of internal defeat, the reason why it is epistemically proper for us to have the defeaters we have is that we stand in some (epistemically proper) psychological relation to them. Of course, since cases of external defeat are cases in which we do not stand in any psychological relation to the relevant defeaters, this story won't work for external defeat. Accordingly, one way of framing the central task for this section is that it aims to develop an account of the conditions under which it is epistemically proper for us to have defeaters when we do not stand in some psychological relation to them. As we will see, this is no easy task, especially for standard versions of virtue epistemology.

With these points in play, here is the order of business for this section. I first argue that cases of external defeat mean trouble for standard versions of virtue epistemology (Section 5.2). To make room for external defeat, the first step is to develop a distinctively functionalist version of virtue epistemology (Section 5.3).

---

and even successful because of ability. What's more, once you come to know, subsequent shots may well be competent and apt. Crucially, however, this is because now you have a defeater for the defeater provided by the testimony.

Section 5.4 introduces the notion of a proficiency, that is, roughly, an ability that in addition has the function of producing successful attempts in certain conditions and argues that some epistemic abilities are also proficiencies. Finally, Section 5.5 argues that the functionalist version of virtue epistemology does allow us to make room for external defeat. In particular, I will argue that the normativity of proficiencies enables us to develop an account of the conditions under which it is epistemically proper for us to have defeaters even when we do not stand in some psychological relation to them.

6.2 The Problem of External Defeat

That the substantive virtue epistemological account of defeat can deal with paradigm cases of defeat is certainly good news. That said, note that all the paradigm cases of defeat we looked at are cases of internal defeat. At the same time, one of the central aims of this Element is to make room for external defeat. Accordingly, the question I want to ask next is whether our virtue epistemological account of defeat can do so and if so how.

Unfortunately, there is reason for pessimism right from the start. To see why, I'd like to begin by looking at three key facts about external defeat.

First, external defeat affects the justificatory status of beliefs. After all, cases of external defeat are cases of *defeat*.

Second, external defeat turns on normative facts. After all, recall that, on the normative view, for defeat to obtain, that is, for defeaters to undermine the competence of attempts, it must be epistemically proper for one to have them. In this way, defeat in general turns on normative facts.[33]

Third, in cases of external defeat, these normative facts aren't normative facts about beliefs one has formed. Otherwise, they wouldn't be cases of *external* defeat. In fact, more generally, the normative facts on which external defeat turns aren't (or at least needn't be) facts about attempts one has made. If this isn't immediately obvious, just consider the radicalised sexist scientists who don't bother to tune into what their female colleagues tell them. That we have a case of external defeat doesn't turn on them attempting to do anything. For instance, to generate a case of external defeat we don't have to suppose that the sexist scientists tried to listen to their female colleagues but failed. Rather, to generate a case of external defeat, it will suffice if our sexist scientists do not

---

[33] Recall that my account is compatible with a hybrid view, according to which the psychological and the normative view each specify a sufficient condition on what it takes for a defeater to undermine justification (Introduction). Crucially, in cases of external defeat, the defeater isn't psychologically registered. This means that, even on the hybrid view, external defeat turns on normative facts.

attempt anything at all. As a result, the normative facts on which external defeat turns aren't (or at least needn't be) facts about attempts one has made.

With these features of external defeat in play, let's turn to some features of virtue epistemology. First, according to virtue epistemology, knowledge and justified belief are identified with categories of telic normativity, to wit, competent and apt belief.

Second, according to virtue epistemology, telic normativity is autonomous. That is to say, it is not encroached upon by other kinds of normativity (Sosa 2021, 40). It may be worth noting that virtue epistemologists hold that telic normativity is autonomous with good reason. An archer's shot that constitutes a heinous murder may nonetheless be a good shot (qua shot). In fact, it may be just as good a shot as a shot that heroically saves a life. Similarly, a heinous belief about how to best implement a fascist regime may still be a good belief (qua belief). In fact, it may be just as good a belief as a heroic belief about how to best implement a democracy. (It is easy enough to see that similar examples can be found for other potentially encroaching types of normativity such as practical or aesthetic normativity.) These considerations suggest that the quality of an attempt (qua attempt) is independent of whatever other normative qualities the attempt may have. Since it is hard to see how this could be unless telic normativity was autonomous, there is excellent reason to think that telic normativity is indeed autonomous.

Third, telic normativity presupposes that the agent has made an attempt (Sosa 2021, 66). After all, whether an attempt is successful, competent, or apt presupposes that an attempt was made. In the epistemic case, this means that telic normativity presupposes that one has formed a belief. After all, whether one's belief is successful, competent, or apt, presupposes that one has indeed formed a belief.

We are now in a position to see exactly why the phenomenon of external defeat means trouble for virtue epistemology. By the first feature of virtue epistemology, justification of belief is identified with a normative category of telic normativity, that is, competence. By the first feature of external defeat, external defeat affects the justificatory status of beliefs. This means that external defeat affects the status of belief as competent. By the second feature of external defeat, external defeat turns on normative facts. Since, additionally, by the second feature of virtue epistemology, telic normativity is autonomous, we get the result that the normative facts on which external defeat turns must be facts of telic normativity. After all, if this weren't the case, the status of belief as competent would turn on normative facts outside of telic normativity. However, this would mean that telic normativity is encroached upon and would thus be incompatible with the autonomy of telic normativity.[34]

---

[34] Note that the argument doesn't really require the autonomy claim. The weaker non-hybridity claim will do. What I mean by 'non-hybridity' is that whether an attempt has some telic normative property, whether it is successful, competent, or apt, turns only on telic normative facts. This is compatible with

By the third feature of external defeat, the normative facts on which external defeat turns aren't normative facts about beliefs one has formed, and, more generally, they aren't (or needn't be) normative facts about attempts one has made. But all of this is incompatible with the third feature of virtue epistemology, according to which telic normativity presupposes that an attempt was made. After all, if the normative facts on which external defeat turns aren't (or needn't be) normative facts about some attempt one has made, then they cannot be facts of telic normativity. And since telic normativity presupposes that an attempt was made, there are no normative facts of telic normativity about attempts one hasn't made.

What comes to light is that virtue epistemology is incompatible with our three key facts about external defeat. By the same token, there is reason to think that virtue epistemology cannot make room for external defeat.

6.3 The Functionalist Account of Abilities

The argument that virtue epistemology cannot make room for external defeat rests on three key features of virtue epistemology. To the extent that virtue epistemologists want to make room in their epistemology for external defeat, they might think again whether they really want to hold on to all three of these claims. Perhaps one of them can be rejected after all, and perhaps this will usher the way towards a viable virtue epistemological account of external defeat.

While I do not mean to deny that this is one way to tackle the issue, it is not the approach I will pursue here. Why not? In a nutshell, this is because I take the crux of the problem for virtue epistemology to be that the normative framework provided by telic normativity is too limited. It is a normative framework for assessing attempts that one has made. However, what we need is a normative framework for assessing attempts one didn't make. And it is far from clear whether the framework can be expanded in any substantive manner beyond attempts one has made and, if so, how this might be done. Instead of trying to amend telic normativity, I want to turn over a new leaf and develop a virtue epistemology from a slightly different starting point. More specifically, I want to start by thinking about the nature and normativity of abilities. The central property of this approach is the property of a function. Accordingly, to see how it works, it will be useful to start by taking a look at what a function is.

The kind of function I am interested in here turns on the existence of a feedback loop involving the functional item and a good functional effect,

---

the falsity of autonomy. For instance, it is compatible with encroachment of other kinds of normativity on telic normativity in the sense that other kinds of normativity partly determine the telic normative facts on which whether an attempt is, say, competent depends. It is easy to see that non-hybridity will be enough to get the above argument off the ground. After all, it will give us the key claim that the normative facts on which external defeat turns must be facts of telic normativity.

which it produces in a system.[35] ('Function' will henceforth refer to this kind of function unless otherwise noted.) The heart is an example of an item with a function (Graham 2012). It is widely recognised that one (if not the) key function of the heart is to pump blood. Why is that? According to the present account, the answer is that pumping blood is good in that it contributes to the proliferation of genes that are responsible for its existence, by keeping us alive long enough to procreate. The fact that the heart pumps blood contributes to explaining why hearts exist which, in turn, contributes to explaining why they continue to pump blood. In this way, hearts exemplify exactly the kind of feedback loop characteristic of functions.

Now, here is the first key idea of the view I am trying to develop: abilities are ways of producing attempts that have the function of producing the relevant kind of success for the agent (henceforth also 'the functionalist account of abilities'[36]). For instance, to have the ability to score free-throws in basketball you must have a way of shooting free-throws that has the function of scoring free-throws for you. Of course, functions are unpacked as expected in terms of a feedback loop, here involving a way of producing attempts and a relevant success, which it produces for the agent: the way of producing attempts explains why the successes are produced and the production of successes explains why the way of producing attempts is in place. In the case of your ability to score free-throws, that you shoot in the way that you do must explain why you score free throws and the fact that you score free-throws must explain why you shoot in the way that you do.[37]

Now, crucially, it is widely agreed that functions have normative import. In particular, their normative import can be read off the answers to the following two questions:

---

[35] The most popular account of this kind of function is the etiological account according to which functions turn on a history of successes. Prominent defences include Godfrey-Smith (1994); Millikan (1984); Neander (1991). For applications to epistemology see, for example, Graham (2012); Simion (2019). That said, a promising alternative is the organisational theory of functions which has been defended in for example, Christensen and Bickhard (2002); McLaughlin (2000).

[36] The perhaps most prominent defender of a functionalist account of abilities is Ruth Millikan (e.g. 2004).

[37] It may be worth noting that the above functionalist account of abilities differs from the standard virtue epistemological account of abilities in at least two important respects. First, according to the standard virtue epistemological account, abilities are analysed in terms of dispositions (e.g. Greco 2010; Sosa 2015), whereas on the functionalist account, they are analysed in terms of functions. Second, according to the standard virtue epistemological account, abilities are properties of agents rather than properties of ways of attempting (Sosa 2015). I have defended both elements of the functionalist account of abilities elsewhere (Kelp 2017, 2018, 2019), and I will not rehearse these arguments here. Instead, I will rest content with exploring the prospects of the functionalist account of abilities for making room for external defeat in a virtue epistemology. If it can do so, this will in itself be a significant enough result, no matter whether, in addition, there is independent reason to think that it is preferable to the standard virtue epistemological account of abilities.

1. Does the functional item fulfil its function?
2. Is the functional item functioning properly?

Regarding function fulfilment, the item meets the first normative standard if and only if the item does produce the functional effect in question. Function fulfilment is rather straightforward.

Things are a little more complex when it comes to proper functioning. To understand this normative standard, we need a bit of conceptual machinery. We have already seen one crucial concept: function fulfilment. The other two are normal functioning and normal conditions. Roughly, normal conditions are the conditions that obtain in the feedback loop in which the functional item produces the functional effect. And, again roughly, normal functioning is the way of functioning that produces the functional effect in the feedback loop, under normal conditions. To make these ideas a little more concrete, consider the heart once more. Here normal conditions include being hooked up to the arteries and veins of a certain kind of organism in a certain way and normal functioning is beating at a certain rate. Functioning normally (beating at a certain rate) under normal conditions (whilst hooked up to arteries and veins), the heart produces its functional effect (pumping blood).

With these points in play, we can now see what proper functioning amounts to for items with functions. In a nutshell, the idea is that proper functioning is normal functioning. When the heart is beating at a certain rate it is functioning properly. In order to figure out whether a functional item is functioning properly, then, we need to ask whether it is functioning normally, that is, whether it is functioning in the way it does when producing the functional effect in the feedback loop, under normal conditions. And, again, the item meets the second normative standard if and only if it is.[38]

Of course, if the functionalist account of abilities holds, then so does the normative import of functions. In particular, we can ask whether, on a given occasion, an ability fulfilled its function and whether it was functioning properly. Since function fulfilment is unpacked in terms of the production of the

---

[38] Earlier on I mentioned that 'proper' signals the presence of some corresponding norm. I left the question as to the precise nature of this norm open (e.g. whether the norm has the force of a 'should', a 'may', or something else entirely). I did say that this question is to be settled by the correct theory of the normative import of functions. Now, in my view, proper functions give rise to norms that have the force of a 'should'. For instance, to say that the heart is functioning properly by beating at a certain rate is to say that the heart should beat at a certain rate. If this is correct, then epistemic norms generated by proper epistemic functioning will also have the force of a 'should'. While I think that this is the right result, I recognise that the point is controversial. Perhaps it is less problematic once we acknowledge that these shoulds are generated by functions in a perfectly familiar way. Even so, this commitment is optional for present purposes in the sense that it may be that functions don't support norms with the force of a 'should'. This is also why I will continue to state the view in terms of 'propriety' and its cognates here.

functional effect and since the functional effects of abilities are successful attempts, we get the result that an ability fulfils its function if and only if the attempt it produces is successful. Moreover, proper functioning is analysed in terms normal functioning, that is, in terms of functioning in the way that produces the functional effect in the feedback loop, under normal conditions. For abilities, normal functioning involves the production of attempts that are in the range of the ability in the way at issue in the ability. After all, that's the kind of functioning that produces the functional effect, that is, successful attempts, under normal conditions. But now note that what we end up with is an account of the normativity of abilities that features normative categories that attempts produced by them satisfy if and only if they are, respectively, successful and competent. In this way, the functionalist account of ability, in conjunction with the normative import of functions, will effectively allow us to recover two out of the three central normative categories of telic normativity.[39,40]

6.4 Proficiencies

The question remains, however, how this functionalist version of virtue epistemology can help with developing an account of external defeat. To answer it, recall what I take to be the crux of the problem with external defeat for virtue epistemology. Telic normativity is a normative framework for attempts that one has made. What we need is a normative framework for attempts one doesn't make. In this way, the normative framework that telic normativity provides is

---

[39] What about aptness, the third category of telic normativity? Perhaps functionalist normativity can be developed to make room for aptness. But note that, on my view, it's not really an issue if this cannot be done. To see why, recall first that while standard virtue epistemology takes the epistemic success of belief to be truth, on my view it is knowledge (Kelp 2016, 2017, 2018, 2021a, 2021b). But, of course, even on the above functionalist view, success is a central normative category, even if we cannot make room for aptness as a central normative category. After all, function fulfilment is a central normative category – in fact, it is the central normative category. And since for an ability to fulfil its function is for it to produce a successful attempt, success is a – and arguably the – central normative category here too. On a knowledge-centric version of virtue epistemology, we don't really need the normative category of aptness to explain the normativity of knowledge and justified belief. We can make do with the categories of success and competence. And since those categories can be recovered by the above functionalist view, the question of whether there is room for aptness as well is of comparatively little consequence, at least for champions of knowledge-centric versions of virtue epistemology. In fact, my own preferred view departs from virtue epistemology in that it abandons aptness as a central normative category and argues that the intuitions supporting the claim that aptness is a central normative category can be given a fully adequate alternative explanation (Kelp 2021a, 2023).

[40] It may be worth noting that the resulting view is similar to proper functionalist accounts of justified belief (e.g. Bergmann 2006; Graham 2012; Plantinga 1993; Simion 2019). Relevant differences include that my view is expressly agent relative (see Kelp (2023) and Section 3, Section 3.5), that it is analyses justification in terms of knowledge, and that it aims to accommodate external defeat (of course, Simion would agree on the last two counts).

limited in scope and it is just not clear whether the framework can be expanded in any substantive manner beyond attempts and, if so, how.

Crucially, functionalist normativity is not limited in scope in this way. After all, we can use functionalist normativity to assess lots of things besides attempts. In this way, functionalist normativity expands beyond attempts. We'll have functions when we have the relevant feedback loop between the functional item and the functional effect, and we have normative import when we have functions. When we saw that we can recover two normative categories of telic normativity in functionalist normativity, what we effectively saw was that (at least a certain part of) telic normativity can be embedded in the broader framework of functionalist normativity. While that is in itself an attractive result, what is most important for present purposes is that the normative framework we are employing is much broader in scope. As a result, its resources are not exhausted by the normativity of attempts, nor by the normativity of abilities. And it is precisely these additional resources that will allow us to make headway towards a better account of external defeat.

How so? To answer this question, I'd first like to distinguish abilities from what I will call proficiencies. To get a better handle on this distinction, consider the basketball case again. Whether you have an ability to make shots with your right, say, in a certain range turns on whether you have a way of shooting that has the function to make shots in that range. Note that while you may have this ability, it may well be that you rarely if ever exercise it. Perhaps this is because you are cautious, perhaps it is because you have taken a vow never to shoot with your right again, or perhaps it is for some other reason entirely. Now contrast this case with a case in which you don't have an ability, but you produce many shots. You are prolific at producing shots and have what we may call a prolificacy. Perhaps the number of successful shots you produce in a day is exactly the same in both cases.

Now, the key suggestion is that proficiencies combine abilities and prolificacies in a certain way. First, any genuine proficiency is also an ability. A mere way of attempting that is not an ability is not a proficiency, not even if it produces successful attempts prolifically. Suppose my way of attempting free-throws is by throwing balls right up in the air. In this case, I don't have a genuine ability to make free throws, not even if I make many free throws, say because there is an army of clandestine helpers with wind machines that see to it that my shots are successful (Kelp 2017, 2018, 2019). Likewise, I don't have a genuine proficiency to make free throws, again no matter whether I happen to make a lot of free-throws.

If a genuine proficiency is also an ability, the question that arises is what more is required for an ability to qualify as a proficiency. One might think that the answer is simply that one exercises one's ability a lot. But, again, this can't be quite right. To see this, consider two agents, A and B, who both have a certain ability. A exercises their ability rarely, but when they do, their attempts are virtually always successful. In contrast, B exercises it frequently but indiscriminately with the result that their attempts are virtually never successful. Let's suppose that A produces successful attempts as often as (or perhaps even more often than) B. While B is more prolific than A, it is not the case that B is more proficient than A. As a result, whether an ability qualifies as a proficiency cannot just be a matter of how often one exercises one's ability. Note also that what it takes for an ability to qualify as a proficiency cannot only turn on whether one exercises one's ability a lot and on whether one frequently succeeds upon exercising one's ability. Again, the fact that one succeeds frequently might be accidental to exercise of the ability in which case the ability isn't a proficiency.

Unsurprisingly, I want to suggest explaining the difference between an ability and a proficiency in functionalist terms. More specifically, at a minimum, a proficiency is an ability that has the function of producing successes across a range of trigger conditions, that is, conditions that trigger the exercise of the ability.[41] Since proficiencies are functional entities, they have normative import. We can ask whether a proficiency fulfilled its function and whether it was functioning properly. Of course, proper functioning here is understood in the expected way in terms of normal functioning, that is, the way of functioning that produces the functional effect in the feedback loop, under normal conditions. For proficiencies, normal functioning involves the obtaining of some trigger conditions, which trigger the exercise of the ability, which produces an attempt, which is successful, at least under normal conditions. The key point here is that normal functioning of the proficiency involves functioning that proceeds from the obtaining of some trigger conditions to the production of an attempt.

Let's look at how these rather abstract points about proficiencies play out in the sorts of epistemic cases that are of central interest here. First, note that many epistemic abilities are also proficiencies. Suppose, for instance, that I am looking at a blue dot on a white background. I have the perceptual ability to recognise blue things: I have a way of forming perceptual beliefs that has the

---

[41] Beyond that, proficiencies come in degrees. In particular, I want to suggest that a maximal proficiency is one that involves a maximal ability, that is, a way of producing attempts that has a maximal success to failure ratio and does so no matter what conditions one may find oneself in. In addition, and more importantly for present purposes, a maximal proficiency is also maximally calibrated to the ability. By this I mean that the conditions under which the ability has the function of producing successes coincides with the conditions under which an attempt produced by the ability would be successful. Degrees of proficiency can then be measured in terms of approximations to maximal proficiencies.

function of producing perceptual knowledge about blue things. However, my perceptual ability is also a proficiency. It has the function of producing perceptual knowledge about blue things across a range of conditions that trigger its exercise. For instance, looking at a blue dot on a white background is among these trigger conditions. My ability to recognise blue things has the function of generating knowledge of the presence of something blue under those conditions ('the blue dot case').

Suppose, next, that I am told that you like Degas. I have the ability to learn from testimony: I have a way of forming testimonial beliefs that has the function of producing testimonial knowledge. At the same time, my testimonial ability is also a proficiency. It has the function of producing testimonial knowledge across a range of trigger conditions. For instance, being told that you like Degas is among these conditions. My ability to learn from testimony has the function of generating knowledge that you like Degas under those conditions ('the Degas case').

In all of these cases, normal functioning of proficiencies involves functioning from the obtaining of some trigger conditions to the production of a belief, which, under normal conditions, qualifies as knowledge. But since normal functioning is proper functioning, the result that we get is that an epistemic proficiency will function properly only if the obtaining of the trigger conditions leads to the formation of a belief. In this way, then, the result that we get is that if the trigger conditions obtain, it is proper for the proficiency to output a belief.

Before moving on to external defeat, I'd like to mention one important point about epistemic proficiencies, that is, that they break down into at least two components. One component involves the uptake of information, the other the formation of beliefs. What I'd like to focus on here is the component involving information-uptake. Note that this is an epistemic proficiency in its own right, which is a constituent of the broader epistemic proficiency that has the function of producing knowledge. Here function fulfilment consists in the uptake of information and normal functioning consists in the functioning from the obtaining of some trigger conditions to the uptake of propositional content (henceforth 'content' for short) that, under normal conditions, qualifies as information.[42] In the blue dot case, my ability to recognise blue is a proficiency with the function of generating knowledge of the presence of blue things via a contained

---

[42] I am taking it that information is at least factive such that one can take up the information that p only if p is true. In cases in which it seems that p but p is false, one cannot take up the information that p. For instance, if the animal before you looks like a zebra but is a cleverly disguised mule, then you cannot take up the information that the animal is a zebra. In this case, I will say that what you take up is the propositional content that the animal is a zebra. A propositional content here, is, very roughly, what the good and the bad case have in common and what, in the good case, qualifies as information.

proficiency to take up information about the presence of blue things. Likewise, in the Degas case, my ability to learn from testimony is a proficiency with the function of generating testimonial knowledge via a contained proficiency to take up testimonial information – here that you like Degas. It is these information-uptake proficiencies that are key to making room for external defeat, as I will explain in what follows.

6.5 External Defeat

With these points on proficiencies and their normative import in play, let's return to external defeat. In what follows, I will outline how proficiencies – and, in particular, information-uptake proficiencies – can pave the way towards a better account of external defeat.

To begin with, note that the norm that corresponds to the proper functioning of information-uptake proficiencies is a genuinely epistemic norm. This is because it derives from a genuinely epistemic function of epistemic proficiencies, that is, ultimately, the production of knowledge that is the function of the proficiencies of which information-uptake proficiencies are constituents (Kelp 2023; Simion 2021).

Second, this epistemic norm is a norm one may fail to live up to without forming any belief or taking up any contents at all. For instance, in the case in which I am looking at a blue dot on a white background, my epistemic ability to perceptually recognise blue things contains a proficiency which, when functioning epistemically properly, will take up the content (and, under normal conditions, the information) that the dot is blue upon being presented with a blue dot on a white background. If I fail to take up the content that the dot is blue, I am in violation of this norm. Similarly, in the testimony case, my ability to learn from testimony involves a proficiency to take up information. When it functions epistemically properly, it will take up the content (and, under normal conditions, the information) that you like Degas upon me being told that you do. If I fail to take up the content that you like Degas, I violate this norm.

Recall what I take to be the crucial problem with external defeat for virtue epistemology, that is, that the normative framework it employs, telic normativity, is too limited in that it doesn't allow us to assess attempts that one hasn't made. We can now see that my distinctively functionalist version of virtue epistemology, in conjunction with proficiencies, allows us to make progress on this problem. This is because the functions of epistemic proficiencies give us norms that are genuinely epistemic and that one may violate without forming beliefs or even taking up any contents at all. And that is exactly what telic normativity-based virtue epistemology failed to do.

Even if we can avoid the crucial problem with external defeat for telic normativity-based virtue epistemology, it remains to be seen that the functionalist alternative can actually deal with the problem. To this end, recall that the virtue epistemological account of defeat I developed in the last section contained three central ideas: first, that in cases of defeat, the ranges of abilities required for justified belief are shifted; second, that defeaters are evidence that attempting (in a certain way) isn't successful; third, that defeaters undermine justification (by shifting ranges of abilities) if and only if it is epistemically proper for one to have them. Recall also that I said that the first and the second key ideas work in exactly the same way for internal and external defeat and that what requires special treatment is the third key idea. In particular, recall that I said that the central task of this section is to develop an account of the conditions under which it is epistemically proper for us to have defeaters when we do not stand in some psychological relation to them.

We are now in a position to see how this task can be accomplished. The crucial claim is that epistemic proper functioning of information-uptake proficiencies corresponds to a way in which it is epistemically proper for one to have this information. For instance, in the blue dot case, when epistemic proper functioning of my proficiency involved with the uptake of information about the presence of blue things will lead me to take up the content (and, under normal conditions, the information) that the dot on the white background I am looking at is blue, it is epistemically proper for me to have the content that the dot is blue. And, in the Degas case, when epistemic proper functioning of my testimonial proficiency will lead me to take up the content (and, under normal conditions, the information) that you like Degas, it is epistemically proper for me to have the content that you like Degas.

We are now in a position to see how we can make room for cases of external defeat in our epistemology. These cases are cases in which it is epistemically proper for one to take up and thus have certain contents that qualify as defeaters, but one does not take up said contents.

By way of illustration, let's return to the case of the racist teacher. Recall that, in this case, a black student raises their hand in class. As a result of racism, the teacher doesn't even register that the black student raised their hand and forms the belief that no one is willing to answer the question. In this case, the teacher's belief that no one is willing to answer the question is clearly not justified. The present account can explain this. In this case, it is epistemically proper for them to take up the information that the black student who raised their hand did indeed raise their hand. This is because their perceptual epistemic abilities are also proficiencies which, when functioning properly, take up the content (and, under normal conditions, the information) that the black student in question raised their hand. But, of course, that the black student in question did raise their hand is a defeater for their belief that no one in the class is willing to answer the question. Since it is epistemically proper for the racist teacher to take up a content that is a defeater for their belief that no one in the class is willing to answer the question, their belief that no one in the class is willing to answer the question suffers from defeat. Since, at the same time, they do not take up the defeater, what we are looking at is a case of external defeat.

In the above case, it is a perceptual proficiency that generates a defeater. It is easy enough to see that other proficiencies can also do so. To see this, let's return to the case of the radicalised sexist scientists who don't even tune into what their female colleagues tell them because they are sexists and their female colleagues who found a flaw with one of their experiments. In this case, the sexist scientists' epistemic ability to learn from testimony is a proficiency, which contains an information-uptake proficiency. When functioning epistemically properly, this information-uptake proficiency will take up the content (and, under normal conditions, the information) that there is a flaw with the experiment based on which they believe that p. As a result, it is epistemically proper for them to take up the content (and, under normal conditions, the information) that there is a flaw with the experiment based on which they believe that p. But, as we have already seen, this means that it is epistemically proper for them to have a defeater for their belief that p. This means that the sexist scientists' beliefs that p suffers from defeat. Since, in this case, the sexist scientists are radicalised and don't even psychologically register the defeater that it is epistemically proper for them to have, the case is another case of external defeat.

What comes to light is that proficiencies support epistemic norms that one can violate without forming beliefs or taking up information. When we fail to have information that, thanks to the existence of a proficiency, it is epistemically proper for us have, we may have cases of external defeat. This happens when the contents that it is epistemically proper for us to have but that we don't have are defeaters. In this way, proficiencies allow us to make room for external defeat in our epistemology.

6.6 Conclusion

In this section, I returned to external defeat. In particular, I have shown how the virtue epistemological account from the previous section can be further developed to make room for external defeat.

To this end, I first argued that standard virtue epistemology faces an in-principle obstacle when it comes to accommodating external defeat. In a nutshell, the trouble is that to make sense of external defeat, we need to countenance epistemic norms governing beliefs one doesn't form or, more generally, attempts that one doesn't make. The problem for standard virtue epistemology is that it cannot do so. This is because the normative framework it employs is a framework evaluating attempts that one has made. It doesn't have the resources to evaluate attempts one doesn't make.

I then sketched an alternative way of understanding the nature and normativity of abilities in terms of functions. I argued that two central categories of telic normativity, that is, success and competence, can be recovered by this view. At the same time, the normative framework that it comes with isn't limited to attempts one has made. In this way, a first step towards overcoming a key obstacle to making room for external defeat is made.

Next, I introduced a distinction between abilities and proficiencies. Very roughly, abilities have to do with the reliability of success: the more reliable you are, the better your ability. Abilities are in an important way independent of the conditions under which attempts are triggered. You can have a strong ability and yet virtually never produce attempts. Again, very roughly, proficiencies are abilities that depend on the conditions under which attempts are triggered. What's key to proficiencies is that they have the function of producing successful attempts under certain trigger conditions. Since they are functional entities, they are governed by the normative import of functions. Most importantly, proficiencies may violate norms of proper functioning even when attempts aren't produced. In this way, we took a second important step towards making room for external defeat.

The last key step was to argue that many epistemic abilities are proficiencies. In particular, they are proficiencies that contain information-uptake proficiencies. Epistemic proper functioning of these proficiencies involves the uptake of content (and, under normal conditions, information) given certain trigger conditions. The epistemic norm of proper functioning is violated when the trigger conditions obtain but no content is taken up. Since this is exactly what happens in cases of external defeat, we have finally succeeded in making room for external defeat in our epistemology.

References

Alston, W. 2002. 'Plantinga, Naturalism, and Defeat'. In *Naturalism Defeated? Essays on Plantinga's Evolutionary Argument against Naturalism*, edited by Beilby, J. Ithaca: Cornell University Press 176–203.

Baker-Hytch, M., and M. A. Benton. 2015. 'Defeatism Defeated'. *Philosophical Perspectives* 29: 40–66.

Beddor, B. 2015. 'Process Reliabilism's Troubles with Defeat'. *Philosophical Quarterly* 65: 145–59.

Beddor, B. 2021. 'Reasons for Reliabilism.' In *Reasons, Justification, and Defeat*, edited by Jessica Brown and Mona Simion, 146–76. Oxford University Press.

Bergmann, M. 2006. *Justification Without Awareness*. Oxford: Oxford University Press.

BonJour, L. 1980. 'Externalist Theories of Empirical Knowledge'. *Midwest Studies in Philosophy* 5: 53–73.

1985. *The Structure of Empirical Justification*. Cambridge, MA: Harvard University Press.

Chisholm, R. 1977. *Theory of Knowledge*. 2nd ed. Englewood Cliffs: Prentice Hall.

Christensen, D., and M. H. Bickhard. 2002. 'The Process Dynamics of Normative Function.' *The Monist* 85: 3–28.

Coates, A. 2012. 'Rational Epistemic Akrasia'. *American Philosophical Quarterly* 49 (2): 113–24.

Comesaña, J. 2005. 'Unsafe Knowledge'. *Synthese* 146: 395–404.

Conee, E., and R. Feldman. 2004. *Evidentialism: Essays in Epistemology*. Oxford: Oxford University Press.

Firth, R. 1978. 'Are Epistemic Concepts Reducible to Ethical Concepts?' In *Values and Morals: Essays in Honor of William Frankena, Charles Stevenson, and Richard Brandt*, edited by A. Goldman and J. Kim, 215–29. Dordrecht: Kluwer Academic Publishers.

Fernández Vargas, M. A. ed. 2016. *Performance Epistemology: Foundations and Applications*. Oxford: Oxford University Press.

Frances, B. 2005. *Scepticism Comes Alive*. Oxford: Oxford University Press.

Fricker, M. 2007. *Epistemic Injustice: Power and the Ethics of Knowing*. Oxford: Oxford University Press.

Gettier, E. 1963. 'Is Justified True Belief Knowledge?' *Analysis* 23: 121–3.

Godfrey-Smith, P. 1994. 'A Modern History Theory of Functions'. *Noûs* 28: 344–62.

Goldberg, S. C. 2018. *To the Best of Our Knowledge: Social Expectations and Epistemic Normativity*. Oxford: Oxford University Press.

Goldman, A. 1979. 'What Is Justified Belief?' In *Justification and Knowledge*, edited by G. Pappas, 1–25. Dordrecht: Reidel.

2012. *Reliabilism and Contemporary Epistemology*. New York/NY: Oxford University Press.

Graham, P. 2012. 'Epistemic Entitlement'. *Noûs* 46: 449–82.

Graham, P. and Lyons, J. 2021. 'The Structure of Defeat: Pollock's Evidentialism, Lackey's Framework, and Prospects for Reliabilism'. In *Reasons, Justification, and Defeat*, edited by Brown, J. and Simion, M. Oxford: Oxford University Press 39–68.

Greco, J. 2010. *Achieving Knowledge*. Cambridge: Cambridge University Press.

2012. 'A (Different) Virtue Epistemology'. *Philosophy and Phenomenological Research* 85: 1–26.

Greco, J., and J. Turri. 2013. 'Virtue Epistemology.' In *The Stanford Encyclopedia of Philosophy*, edited by E.N. Zalta, Winter 2013. http://plato.stanford.edu/archives/win2013/entries/epistemology-virtue/.

Harman, G. 1980. 'Reasoning and Evidence One Does Not Possess'. *Midwest Studies in Philosophy* 5: 163–82.

Hetherington, Stephen Cade 2001. *Good Knowledge, Bad Knowledge: On Two Dogmas of Epistemology*. New York: Oxford University Press.

Kelp, C. 2009. 'Knowledge and Safety'. *Journal of Philosophical Research* 34: 21–31.

2016. 'Justified Belief: Knowledge First-Style'. *Philosophy and Phenomenological Research* 93: 79–100. https://doi.org/10/grpk2f.

2017. 'Knowledge First Virtue Epistemology.' In *Knowledge First: Approaches in Epistemology and Mind*, edited by A. Carter, E. Gordon, and B. Jarvis. Oxford: Oxford University Press 223–245.

2018. *Good Thinking: A Knowledge First Virtue Epistemology*. London: Routledge.

2019. 'How to Be a Reliabilist'. *Philosophy and Phenomenological Research* 98: 346–74. https://doi.org/10.1111/phpr.12438.

2021a. *Inquiry, Knowledge, and Understanding*. Oxford: Oxford University Press.

2021b. 'Theory of Inquiry'. *Philosophy and Phenomenological Research* 103: 359–84. https://doi.org/10.1111/phpr.12719.

2023. 'Agent Functionalism'. In *The Blackwell Companion to Epistemology*, edited by K. Sylvan. Oxford: Wiley-Blackwell.

Kelp, C., and J. Greco. 2020. *Virtue Theoretic Epistemology: New Methods and Approaches*. Cambridge: Cambridge University Press.

Kelp, C., and M. Simion. 2021. *Sharing Knowledge: A Functionalist Account of Assertion*. Cambridge: Cambridge University Press.

2023. 'What Is Normative Defeat?' *Manuscript*.

Kornblith, H. ed. 2001. *Epistemology: Internalism and Externalism*. Oxford: Blackwell.

Lackey,J. 1999. 'Testimonial Knowledge and Transmission'. *Philosophical Quarterly* 49: 471–90.

2003. 'A Minimal Expression of Non-Reductionism in the Epistemology of Testimony'. *Noûs* 37: 706–23.

2008. *Learning from Words: Testimony as a Source of Knowledge*. Oxford: Oxford University Press.

2018. 'Credibility and the Distribution of Epistemic Goods.' In *Believing in Accordance with the Evidence*, edited by K. McCain. Dordrecht: Springer 145–168.

Lasonen-Aarnio, M. 2010. 'Unreasonable Knowledge'. *Philosophical Perspectives* 24: 1–21.

2014. 'Higher-Order Evidence and the Limits of Defeat'. *Philosophy and Phenomenological Research* 88: 314–45.

Lehrer, K. 1990. *Theory of Knowledge*. London: Routledge.

Lehrer, K., and T. D. Paxson. 1969. 'Knowledge: Undefeated Justified True Belief'. *Journal of Philosophy* 66: 225–37.

Lyons, J. 2009. *Perception and Basic Beliefs: Zombies, Modules, and the Problem of the External World*. Oxford: Oxford University Press.

McLaughlin, P. 2000. *What Functions Explain: Functional Explanation and Self-Reproducing Systems*. Cambridge: Cambridge University Press.

Millikan, R. 1984. *Language, Thought, and Other Biological Categories*. Cambridge, MA: MIT Press.

2004. *Varieties of Meaning*. Cambridge, MA: MIT Press.

Neander, K. 1991. 'Functions as Selected Effects: The Conceptual Analyst's Defence'. *Philosophy of Science* 58: 168–84.

Neta, R., and G. Rohrbaugh. 2004. 'Luminosity and the Safety of Knowledge'. *Pacific Philosophical Quarterly* 85: 396–406.

Nottelmann, N. 2021. 'Against Normative Defeat'. *Mind* 130: 1183–1204.

Plantinga, A. 1993. *Warrant and Proper Function*. Oxford: Oxford University Press.

2000. *Warranted Christian Belief*. Oxford: Oxford University Press.

Pollock, J. L. 1986. *Contemporary Theories of Knowledge*. London: Hutchinson.

Pritchard, D. 2005. *Epistemic Luck*. Oxford: Oxford University Press.

Shah, N. 2006. 'A New Argument for Evidentialism'. *The Philosophical Quarterly* 56: 481–98.

Silva, P., and L. Oliveira. eds. 2022. *Propositional and Doxastic Justification: New Essays on Their Nature and Significance*. London: Routledge.

Simion, M. 2019. 'Knowledge-First Functionalism'. *Philosophical Issues* 29: 254–67.

2023. 'Resistance to Evidence and the Duty to Believe'. *Philosophy and Phenomenological Research*. https://doi.org/10.1111/phpr.12964

Sosa, E. 1999. 'How to Defeat Opposition to Moore'. In *Philosophical Perspectives*, edited by J. Tomberlin, 137–49. Oxford: Blackwell.

2015. *Judgment and Agency*. Oxford: Oxford University Press.

2021. *Epistemic Explanations. A Theory of Telic Normativity, and What It Explains*. Oxford: Oxford University Press.

Sartwell, Crispin 1992. 'Why Knowledge Is Merely True Belief'. *Journal of Philosophy* 89 (4):167–80.

Swain, M. 1974. 'Epistemic Defeasibility'. *American Philosophical Quarterly* 11: 15–25.

Turri, John 2012. 'Is Knowledge Justified True Belief?' *Synthese* 184 (3): 247–59.

Wedgwood, R. 2012. 'Justified Inference'. *Synthese* 189 (2): 273–95.

Williamson, T. 2000. *Knowledge and Its Limits*. Oxford: Oxford University Press.

Williamson, T. 2009. 'Replies to Critics.' In *Williamson on Knowledge*, edited by D. Pritchard and P. Greenough, 279–384. Oxford: Oxford University Press.

Zagzebski, L. 1996. *Virtues of the Mind: An Inquiry into the Nature of Virtue and the Ethical Foundations of Knowledge*. Cambridge: Cambridge University Press.

Zimmermann, M. 1997. 'Moral Responsibility and Ignorance'. *Ethics* 107: 410–26.

Funding Statement

The research for this book is supported by a grant from the European Research Council under the European Union's Horizon 2020 research and innovation programme (grant agreement n° 948356).

Cambridge Elements ⁼

Epistemology

Stephen Hetherington

University of New South Wales, Sydney

Stephen Hetherington is Professor Emeritus of Philosophy at the University of
New South Wales, Sydney.
He is the author of numerous books, including *Knowledge and the Gettier Problem*
(Cambridge University Press, 2016) and *What Is Epistemology?* (Polity, 2019), and is the
editor of several others, including *Knowledge in Contemporary Epistemology* (with Markos
Valaris: Bloomsbury, 2019) and *What the Ancients Offer to Contemporary Epistemology* (with
Nicholas D. Smith: Routledge, 2020). He was the Editor-in-Chief of the Australasian Journal
of Philosophy from 2013 until 2022.

About the Series

This Elements series seeks to cover all aspects of a rapidly evolving field, including emerging
and evolving topics such as: fallibilism; knowing-how; self-knowledge; knowledge of
morality; knowledge and injustice; formal epistemology; knowledge and religion;
scientific knowledge; collective epistemology; applied epistemology; virtue epistemology;
wisdom. The series demonstrates the liveliness and diversity of the field, while also
pointing to new areas of investigation.

Cambridge Elements $^{\equiv}$

Epistemology

Elements in the Series

A full series listing is available at: www.cambridge.org/EEPI

Printed in the United States
by Baker & Taylor Publisher Services